JOY DIVISION

AND THE MAKING OF
UNKNOWN PLEASURES

JOY DIVISION

AND THE MAKING OF
UNKNOWN PLEASURES

JAKE KENNEDY

The publisher wishes to thank the Book Division at Lasgo Chrysalis London
for their ongoing support in developing this series.

Published by Unanimous Ltd.
Unanimous Ltd. is an imprint of MQ Publications Ltd.
12 The Ivories, 6–8 Northampton Street, London, N1 2HY

Printed and bound in France

ISBN: 1-903318-80-7

1 2 3 4 5 6 7 8 9

Picture credits:
Cover: © Kevin Cummins/Idols.
Picture section: page 1 © Lex Van Rossen/Redferns; page 2 © Harry
Goodwin/Rex Features; page 3 © Martin O'Neill/Redferns; pages 4 (both), 5
(both), 6, 7, 8 © Kevin Cummins/Idols.

contents

acknowledgments

Deep thanks for helping are more than due to Mick Middles (above and beyond), Anthony H. Wilson, Bernard Sumner, Peter Saville, Richard Searling, Marc Riley, Ian Brown, Chris Hewitt, Alan Hempstall, Henry Yates, Ian Shirley, Michael Eastwood (damn deadlines), Chris Warren, William Perez, Tim Burgess, Jessica Penfold, Marko at LWTUA, Peter Wadsworth, Hardeep Phull, Mike Evans, Sarah-Jane, Ken Hunt, Joel McIver, Daryl Easlea, Andy Davis, Tim Jones, Jason Draper (for offering all he could), Jono Scott, Adam Ryan (for the info on Curtis' former life) and all the fans who agreed to help me with their reminiscences.

Thanks to Keri for making the tea.

The following publications have also been vital to my research and are quoted throughout: *From Joy Division To New Order* (Mick Middles, Virgin), *Unknown Pleasures* (Chris Ott, Continuum), *Joy Division + New Order: Pleasures And Wayward Distractions* (Brian Edge, Omnibus), *Joy Division* (Neil Woodvine, private printing), *Touching From A Distance* (Deborah Curtis, Faber & Faber), *Form And Substance* (Clinton Heylin and Craig Wood, Sound), *24 Hour Party People* (Tony Wilson, MacMillan), *True Faith* (Dave Thompson, Helter Skelter), *Album: Classic Sleeve Design* (Nick De Ville, Mitchell Beazley), *Punk Diary* (George Gimarc, Backbeat), *The Guinness Rockopedia* (Guinness), *Time Travel* (Jon Savage, Chatto &

Windus) and *The All Music Guide* (Backbeat). I am also grateful to countless periodicals, both from the period in discussion and the present day. These include *NME*, *Melody Maker*, *Sounds*, *Mojo*, *Manchester Evening News*, *Select*, *Uncut*, *Zig Zag*, *City Life*, *The Face*, *The Wire*, *Vox* and *Record Collector*.

For website information, I would urge your cursor to visit either the Shadowplay site, at www.lwtua.free-online.co.uk/shadowplay/joy, or the Joy Division Central site at www.members.aol.com/lwtua/joydiv.htm

For those interested in both New Order and Joy Division, I recommend www.worldinmotion.net, or the www.neworderonline.com official band site.

More general information on the Factory label is well documented, but http://home.dialix.com/~u3336/factory/index2.html was most helpful in my research.

Most importantly, this book is dedicated and due in no small part to Jack Kane, a personal inspiration who left us way too early and who could easily have written a book himself (most likely about The Cardiacs). I'm sure anyone who knew him will be aware of the parallels contained herein, and his death was no less a tragedy.

Spero meliora as well, friend, *spero meliora*. I was always on your side.

All for Keri

preface:
where will it end?

This is not a book about death. Certainly, lyrical or musical themes contained within may touch upon such notions, and there are Joy Division fans aplenty obsessed with the morbid side to their music and the tragedy in the short life of singer Ian Curtis. But this book is not about any of that.

When I started to write, I wanted to trace the origins of *Unknown Pleasures*, to try and decode its genetic make-up and to understand the headspace of the four (or five) men who made it, back in 1978 and 1979. I wanted to discern why an album that had affected me from such a young age, such a heavy or 'depressing sounding' record, still found space on my mental playlist some 25 years after it was made.

I wasn't alone. In the year work started on this book (2005), Joy Division were nominated for best song of the last 25 years at the Brit Awards (for 'Love Will Tear Us Apart'), and were widely in the public eye for the anniversary of Curtis' suicide. A film of his life was also well into production (for release in 2006), and many of the interviewees I spoke to during my research told me of four or five other books about the band in various stages of production. The difference with this book is that I wanted to concentrate on the music. I'm not sure the mystique of *Unknown Pleasures* will ever be entirely unwound but I'm fine with that.

A note on the time span in this book

This book deals with the music made around the time of Joy Division's debut album, *Unknown Pleasures*. The cut-off point for inclusion is the last recording session for the album, in mid-April 1979 at Strawberry Studios, Stockport, which means that everything after the Sordide Sentimental 'Licht Und Blindheit' single of March 1980 is left out.

Songs that were released later, either as b- or a-sides or album tracks, are discussed if they were recorded within this time span ('Transmission', for instance). Events and concerts outside that period are also taken into consideration if they are relevant to the music in question.

a beginning

"I remember when we were young"

"Taking a song and making it call you, letting it take control, giving you the opportunity to fill your dreams, or it could stop the world—Joy Division were this realm; independent, their connection to the public was and is more than just rhythmic, with a dynamic rarely attained. One that they commanded. Yet few, so few, were fortunate enough to actually see them perform live"

William Perez, bassist in Joy Revision, Los Angeles

Social class is not a topic that you might expect to open a discussion of Joy Division. But delve into the dim and distant pasts of the four members, their surroundings, or even just the geography of their upbringing, and the long-entrenched attitudes of a city and its suburbs bubble up to the surface.

The Cheshire town of Macclesfield, where Ian Kevin Curtis (born 15 July 1956) was brought up, is not the rough diamond of Salford, or the luscious, sweeping, hills of nearby wealthy Altrincham or Mere (to the south of Manchester). Rather, it falls between the two stools: industrial and urban but with a beautiful countryside just a few minutes drive away. Curtis then would have been continually aware of the possibility of escape.

"Macclesfield's a funny place," says Manchester author and journalist Mick Middles. "It's a very working class town, yet it's surrounded by one of the richest areas in Britain, so it's a mixture of really rich and really poor. It's always been quite raucous of a Saturday night. But it's weird, because they say Ian grew up in a grim area, and he did, but two miles down the road were some of the most beautiful villages in Cheshire. So he wasn't living in the heart of Salford.

"Another thing I remember is that there were no heavy metal bands in Manchester, but there were in Macclesfield. Bikers' pubs and that. It was that sort of area, and still is."

A move to the Victoria Park area of Macclesfield would doubtless have made the idea of escape more appealing to Curtis, as the area lies in the very center of the town. Stephen Morris (b. 28 October 1957) also lived there as a youngster, and the two went to the King's School ("an unusually diverse mixture of people with and without money," according to Middles); Curtis won a scholarship to attend there.

It was at King's School that Curtis met Deborah Woodruffe, marrying her at the age of 19 (on 23 August 1975 in Henbury) while they were both still at the school. In May 1977, after spells of living in Hulme and later Chadderton, the couple moved into a terraced house in Macclesfield. The house—including the triangular room which Ian is reported to have painted sky blue and in which many of his lyrics were written—still stands but is privately owned.

After a life of education spent performing rather than excelling, Curtis moved a step closer to his dreams of musical stardom when he got a job as an assistant in Rare Records, a shop in Manchester's city center. A blossoming interest in the works of David Bowie, Iggy Pop and other bands that sustained a generation not content to be hippies, was fed by simply being in a room where music was the main purpose for existence.

Unlike the Macclesfield of Curtis' youth, Manchester's Salford district offered no prospects of escape. Industrial buildings still lie all around, obscuring the horizon, and remnants of the city's history as a once-bustling port and merchant-house area loom large. It was against this backdrop that Peter Hook (b. 13 February 1956) and Bernard (Barney) Sumner (aka Albrecht or Dickens, b. 4 January 1956) would have been making the best of it. To call them streetwise lads is perhaps going over the top, but compared to their future vocalist, their side of the tracks was distinctly less pretty.

"The Salford thing is obviously important," says Middles. "It helped the dynamic of the band. But I don't think there was a split—most people wouldn't know where Macclesfield was really. It's weird because it [Macclesfield] doesn't know whether it's in the North or the Midlands—it's in the middle of everywhere."

From mid-1976 to the end of that year, Sumner and Hook rehearsed together in a creative period affectionately described by Hook as "crap". They auditioned various school friends as singers and drummers, but none stayed the course. Unsure of their sound and their own ability, they were reluctant to approach the moody-looking guy they'd seen at Pistols gigs—the fact he was already in a band daunted the pair somewhat. But Curtis made it known to the pair that his band—an outfit as embryonic as that of Hook and Sumner—had split. Within a matter of days the trio were rehearsing together in the Black Swan pub in Salford.

It's always hard to pinpoint the exact beginning of a revolution. Revolution, in fact, might be too strong a word. But the life of Joy Division might be traced back to one of two punk events. Some would say the recording of Buzzcocks' *Spiral Scratch* EP was pivotal in prompting Ian Curtis to form, or join, a band worthy of his Iggy- and Bowie-fueled dreams. The physical product, after all, is a great incentive. To hold a seven-inch record in your hand—one produced and funded by lads from your home town—is a powerful experience. It opens up a world of possibilities. If they can do it, so can you.

As 'Breakdown', 'Time's Up', 'Boredom' and 'Friends Of Mine' scratched out from Curtis' speakers, it's not difficult to imagine what must have been going through his mind. Awe, certainly. Envy, perhaps. But more insistent than either of those would be a drive to do the same.

But there was an earlier event that might have instilled a more profound urge in him to get in the studio, or at least on stage—the city's first significant punk event, on 20 July 1976.

Manchester's Lesser Free Trade Hall could be hired for £32 in 1976. Not a massive amount, but enough that you'd feel the pinch. Buzzcocks doubtless did, for they hired the hall twice. The first booking was for 12 June 1976, to put on a gig by the Sex Pistols. Buzzcocks fully intended to be the support act for these punk royals, quite a lofty ambition for their debut gig, but 'personnel problems' meant this wasn't to be (although the gig went on without them).

But by the time of the second booking, word had traveled and the crowd contained a soon-to-be stellar line-up. As well as Ian and Deborah Curtis, Morrissey, Johnny Marr, Tony Wilson, Bernard Sumner and Peter Hook watched the two acts (with Slaughter & The Dogs between them), in a state of shock, as excellently documented in the movie 24 *Hour Party*

People. Wilson, ever the entrepreneur, would offer the head-liners a slot on his *So It Goes* show that night.

Not everyone who says they were there can be believed. Alan Hempstall, vocalist with hippies-turned-punks and Factory signings Crispy Ambulance, remembers the gig somewhat ruefully.

"The gig that New Order and Morrissey were at was the *second* gig. Everyone says they went out the next day and bought a guitar, but it didn't happen that way. I thought they [Sex Pistols] were a great band, and I talked to John Rotten for a couple of minutes, but I was a hippy. Quite honestly, I went back home to my Hawkwind albums! It was only two years later when I really got the buzz, when new wave came about."

But the various members of Manchester's soon-to-be musical elite in attendance were at least spurred on to do something. Peter Hook, it is widely reported, rushed out the next day to buy a cheap bass guitar. Curtis' fire, too, would surely have been lit. After all, he had already been sounding out various school friends and associates for months with a view to forming a band.

If nothing else at this stage in his career, Curtis had drive. Towards what exactly may still have been unclear, but there are reports of him mooching around the RCA offices in Manchester's Piccadilly area, run by area manager Richard Brandwood. RCA was home to Lou Reed and David Bowie, so in a way, just being in those offices took him one step closer to the stardom he desired. Brandwood may not have been able to offer him a deal, or even see anything like a star quality in him at that time, but he didn't kick him out, and Curtis became almost a part of the furniture.

Another formative event in the shy boy's life was when he approached Buzzcock Howard Devoto at a gig in the city. Curtis would later confess that he found the experience slightly disappointing, that Devoto had been too normal and not 'pop starry' enough, that he was too down to earth. Perhaps he had illusions of meeting a Ziggy Stardust-type alien, or even a drugged-out Lou Reed character. Conversely, perhaps such a meeting showed him how it was possible to achieve the goals he was hoping for without being so far removed from the everyday—being grounded in reality, however bleak. Was that not punk's ethos writ large?

Throughout early 1977, the band that became known as Warsaw was practising in a pub called the Black Swan in Salford. Their earlier, contentious, Stiff Kittens moniker has uncertain origins, even to this day. Certain parties blame Buzzcocks, or their manager Richard Boon. Most are certain it was never taken seriously, despite making it to a handful of well-placed concert posters, much to the annoyance of Warsaw. Any reservations about the name are understandable—it is stupid and unbefitting of a band as solemn as Joy Division—but at the time this four-piece was not the same band, and acts like Slaughter & The Dogs were gaining exposure. Different times, then.

Warsaw, as a name, has a certain aura to it. It's well known that the title came from a track ('Warsawa') on the ambient, Brian Eno-produced, second side of David Bowie's essential *Low* album. Hymnal and brooding, the track conjures up a grandeur that must have appealed to the band. But also there was the sense of the iron curtain, of pacts and ice-cold weather, of long coats and fur hats.

When the band supported Buzzcocks at Manchester's Electric Circus venue on 29 May 1977, Sumner, Curtis and Hook were joined by Tony Tabac on drums. Tabac's tenure was shortlived, and listening to the band's musical progression, and to the drummer they later settled on, it's clear that Tabac's rock stylings would not have suited Warsaw, let alone Joy Division.

In June the band played The Squat and the Rafters club, where Wythenshawe-born Rob Gretton was a DJ. Mick Middles: "The Squat is deeply entrenched in history because a lot of people on the edge in the early 1970s, stand-ups like Rik Mayall, would perform there, so it evolved from that. It was a mess. It was as horrible as you could imagine. Rotting floorboards, the beer was rubbish, you couldn't see—perfect really, for a punk venue."

It was at the Rafters gig that the group first struck Gretton as one he felt destined to be involved with. Middles sets the scene…

"Rafters was quite smart by 1977 standards. It was a cellar, and it used to be a folk club in the great days of people like Mike Hardin and Bob Williams, when they used to have folk nights. They had modern, disco nights there too. It was a long, thin place with alcoves down the sides and the stage at the back. If somebody big played there, like Magazine, it was difficult to see. You literally had to hang from the rafters—it was well named."

Would Gretton have been playing his beloved Iggy Pop or The Velvet Underground, bands that Warsaw were already drawing from?

"Well, yes, Gretton did play that. But he also played

Television, and then that reggae crossover, and then a nice bit of Northern soul, so there was always that streak there. He was a skinhead in the early days, so there was a lot of soul. He also played at Pips disco, which was where the first ever Joy Division gig was as Joy Division. It was a good night, but Ian Curtis himself couldn't get in. The bouncers wouldn't let him in." (Curtis eventually made it into the venue just in time for the gig, but only after the other band members had persuaded the over-zealous security men that he really was their singer.)

The Fall's Marc Riley remembers that Warsaw, and Joy Division after them, played frequently in the city at that time. "The first time I saw them they were called Warsaw. Rob Gretton was the DJ at Rafters, so it did seem that Joy Division/Warsaw were *always* on as a support band. It's well known that Rob used to wangle them on. Why wouldn't you? So later, when the opportunity arose, he'd put Joy Division on. So you'd get in there and ask who the support were, and they'd tell you Warsaw, and you'd be 'God, not again.' So people ask me if I ever saw Joy Division and I say, 'Did I ever!' I saw Warsaw probably about 20 times, and Joy Division maybe ten. They did always seem to be on."

In late 1977 Steve Brotherdale joined on drums for the EP *An Ideal For Living*. He was hijacked from a group called Panik, whom Rob Gretton managed. Mick Middles illustrates perfectly why the union might not have been an ideal one.

"I remember Rob Gretton saying 'We've tried out several drummers and one of them was that bastard from the Panik.' He [Brotherdale] was the kind of guy who would go to the phone and pretend to ring his agent. He was with V2 for a while; all the bands he worked with said the same thing about him. It just wouldn't have worked with Joy Division."

It was after this, in response to an advert in a local newspaper, that Stephen Morris joined.

On 2 October the Electric Circus venue in Manchester closed, and to mark its passing there was a weekend party with a number of leading punk bands from the city. A commemorative album (*Short Circuit*) was put together from performances recorded at this mini-festival, with Warsaw contributing 'At A Later Date'. Other acts on the weekend's bill included Slaughter & The Dogs, The Fall, V2, The Negatives and Buzzcocks. To this day, when recollecting the great lost venues of Manchester, an ex-punk from the north will insist the Electric Circus was *the* venue.

"I think the Electric Circus was something special," says Chris Hewitt of Ozit Records, "whereas I think the Factory/Russell Club (*see Chapter Two*) was a bit of a dive and happened for a short period of time, like all the venues."

Mick Middles: "The [Electric] Circus was the ultimate punk venue. It was in a bombsite area of north Manchester that was impossible to get to without being attacked several times, especially if you had drainpipe jeans on. It was like a demolition site. There were modern flats opposite, like jagged teeth, and kids used to stand and lob bricks at the queue waiting to get in. But it was also because of that that it was the best venue in Manchester. It was an old bingo hall, a dangerous place—any fire, or anything like that, would have wiped out the Manchester punk scene."

The release of *An Ideal For Living* in December marked that point in a band's life when suddenly there is a product to push to the punters, something other than hopes and dreams to hide behind. As Chapter Five details, there is little on the recording to signify the Joy Division of the future—even the note included when it was first sent out said the band didn't like the sound—but nevertheless it was out there. Released as both a Warsaw and a Joy Division record, it was a useful enough opening to a career which would develop far beyond it.

The name Joy Division was taken from a novel about a Nazi concentration camp, called *House Of Dolls*, by Karol Cetinsky. There was a London-based band already gigging under the name of Warsaw Pakt; they never actually voiced displeasure at such a similar name, but Warsaw's decision to change was would have been inspired by the individuality of punk, the desire not to be like anyone else. Apart from war-time novel writers, that is.

The actual 'joy division' was supposedly a nickname for the area set aside for female captives who were to be purely of use (in the worst sense) by prison guards and staff. Curtis would also read an extract from the book in a stark monotone during the track 'No Love Lost', but it seems a shame, and somewhat unreasonable, that the music press jumped so quickly to tar the band with the Nazi brush.

Certainly, the choice of name was clumsy. True, these were more 'right on' times than the preceding punk years, but surely the talk of Curtis' fascination with extremes would hint to anyone willing to look beyond the headlines that the choice of name was probably an old-fashioned punk exercise, a matter of old habits dying hard.

Perhaps the young group, who have always had a slightly dismissive attitude to the origins of their band names, were simply young, impetuous and ultimately naïve—as good a summing up of punk as anything in their story. Even so the phrase, if distanced from its history, has a certain bleak grandeur that sadly has been overlooked.

The first gig for the newly named Joy Division was on 25 January 1978 at Pips disco in Manchester. As befitted the time, there were riots.

Nearly three months later, on 14 April, Joy Division played at Manchester's Rafters club, where Granada TV presenter/reporter Anthony Wilson and DJ Rob Gretton were in attendance. Their presence was not unusual, and the two had become friendly over the months. Gretton was the DJ for the venue, revered for his refusal to play requests and for his musical tastes (and contacts), while Wilson was reported to feel more relaxed there, away from the minor celebrity hassles he received at other venues because of his day job.

In his book *From Joy Division To New Order*, Mick Middles recalls that the venue suited Joy Division's sound much better. "[They] seemed curiously suited to Rafters. Their sound gained intensity within those walls, whereas even at the [Electric] Circus, some of the power would evaporate into the surrounding space."

In May the band recorded what is now regarded as the Warsaw/Joy Division 'demo' tape for the RCA label. The session, at Arrow Studios, was funded by northern soul DJ Richard Searling, under the banner of his soul reissue imprint, Grapevine. Searling looks back on those early sessions with what can only be termed fond melancholy.

"My first involvement with Warsaw was when I was working for RCA in 1976. We opened a promotions office in

Manchester. One of our artists was a guy called Iggy Pop, and obviously we had people like Bowie on the label, so I guess just out of inquisitiveness Ian Curtis used to drop by. I don't even know how he found out we were there, because it wasn't exactly on a main street. Nonetheless, we got to know him quite well."

The oddity of a Warsaw record on a soul label was not lost on Searling. But his business partner, Jon Anderson, had brought him into contact with a label luminary of a different age.

"Jon used to spend a lot of time out in America, and his main contact was a guy called Bernie Binnick, a legend, owner of the legendary Swan record label in the US, who'd signed The Beatles. (*Swan licensed the 'She Loves You' single for the US.*) Bernie said that new wave was taking off over there, get us a band for chrissakes, because Henry Stone at TK Records in Miami wanted one. Jon asked me, and I didn't know anyone. But as it happened, there were these dudes in Manchester called Warsaw. They'd been up at Pennine Studios in Rochdale, and they seemed like pretty good guys, so I thought maybe we could do something with them."

The exact details of the deal that was struck remain sketchy but it is important to remember that Searling, as he is at pains to stress, stumped up the cash for the sessions at a time when Warsaw were unloved.

"These guys couldn't get arrested. Nobody wanted to know. They cut a record under the name Warsaw, pressed a thousand, sold about 18. In the course of conversation they asked me what they could do with the other 982. I only say this because nobody, and I know what people say in hindsight, none of the clever buggers like Tony Wilson, none of them wanted to know."

Searling's recollections of the band are telling, illustrating Curtis' excitement at the prospect of being label mates with Bowie and Iggy, and the more canny Hook's suspicion. They also reveal something of an 'on the hoof' nature to the events, which has perhaps not been spelled out previously.

"We went into the studios [Arrow] in Manchester. Ian was very keen, Bernard was 80 per cent keen, Hooky thought we were idiots, which perhaps we were, and Steve the drummer just went along with it. Hooky was worried because he didn't think we had a proper publishing contract, which we probably didn't. The contracts we got weren't particularly good, because that wasn't what we did. We'd never cut anybody in our lives before. Anything we issued on our label was always some American artist that had died years before. We just picked up the master tape and whacked it out. They [the band] looked at us quizzically and wondered who the hell they were getting involved with. But they saw that there wasn't anything else happening for them, and we were shelling out three grand."

Three thousand pounds on a new band is a lot even by today's standards, but in the late 1970s, with Searling reportedly siphoning from his family's holiday fund to illustrate the point, £3,000 was a hell of a lot of money. Searling resumes the story in the studio.

"In we went, and they came in with some songs—'Transmission' I remember. [But] they just seemed to be another Manchester band. However, as soon as we started to get in with them, all these other people started to come out of the woodwork, saying that they knew they were going to make it, and that they were going to do the same."

Searling may have a residual, if faint, bitterness about the groundswell of interest in Warsaw/Joy Division at the time, but it truly seems to be something paternal. But in stark contradiction to other reports of the sessions running into trouble (it has been written that the session manager, Searling's partner Jon Anderson, was seen to argue vehemently and at length with the band, leaving sessions in bitter silence), Searling remembers no cross words or tense stand-offs.

"The sessions were great. I got really good at playing pool, I left it all to Jon Anderson. I seem to remember it was a four-day session. On the first day the tracks were laid in an unbelievably short space of time. They sounded great. Day two was the vocals, and day three was the vocals. Ian, God rest his soul, was struggling with them, for whatever reason, although he came through in the end. He turned it round and sounded great. They did a cover of N.F. Porter's 'Keep On Keepin' On'..."

Yes. You read that right. In some kind of misplaced ambition, the idea had been to fuse the disparate worlds of new wave and soul, presumably with a view to doubling the audience figures. It may seem ridiculous now, but Searling remembers the track making it to completion.

"They recorded it, and we swanned off with the tapes and a few cassettes at the end of the week. We played it to a few people and most thought it was good. Very good. So we thought, right, let's get RCA on the case. Logical—get the A&R people up, fantastic. They dithered for a bit and then said they were gonna go with it. It must have been maybe six weeks after the sessions. Then Rob Gretton got involved..."

The menace of the meddling manager may seem to loom here, but it seems that DJ Gretton, now managing the band after another ex-drummer, Terry Mason, had had difficulty finding gigs for them, really only had their best interests at heart in the 'interruptions' that followed. (Mason, another school friend, had taken over from Tony Tabac, but his drumming had been at best passable, never completely suited to the machine-like sound the band eventually settled on.)

Searling: "I'd no problem with him whatsoever. He seemed like a perfectly good guy, but as soon as he got involved, he basically said that it all needed remixing, that it was a load of crap, that they couldn't do anything with it. Well, we told him that RCA were interested, but he said, 'Don't matter. Major label? Not right for the band.' It was a bit of a stalemate really.

"About a year later we made our one mistake: everything drifted, we weren't gonna be able to work with them again because we weren't on the same wavelength, there were still many bands in Manchester, and [we had] no guarantee [Warsaw] were any different. So, although we knew there was a buzz and they were having their photographs taken in front of weird techno buildings, we let it go."

Here Searling seems honest about the events that were unfolding. As businessmen, he and Anderson may have made the right move. But even so, they might have been better to wait, even just a few months, before selling the tapes. But as the northern soul DJ points out, new wave was just not his thing.

"On a Monday night at the Portland Bars in Manchester, which has been well documented, they gave us the money for the tapes. That was probably not the most sensible thing for us to have done really, but at the time, honestly, you couldn't have called it. It's just the way it is. In 1981 loads of Wigan Casino DJs sold all their soul records because they thought it had died with the venue, but now the records they sold for £80 are worth ten grand! It's just the way it is.

"We got our money back. We gave the tapes back—we could have been bloody-minded and kept them. We did respect their wishes. I think we were enriched by the experience. It probably wouldn't have worked with us: we hadn't got the time to spend developing them. At the end of the day, I'm still proud to have been associated with them."

In late 1978, the Russell Club in Manchester became The Factory on Fridays. Peter Saville, an innovative art and design student who had accosted Tony Wilson at a gig earlier that year, designed the posters for the regular night.

Leading up to these nights, Joy Division rehearsed, were photographed, and generally just hung out in a converted warehouse studio space in Knott Hill, Manchester. The owner of this space was Tony Davidson, the owner of the TJM label, famous for its early backing of Simply Red's Mick Hucknall (it released records by his first band, The Frantic Elevators) along with singles by The Distractions and Manchester punks like V2.

The rooms were lofty, almost cathedral-like, spaces and were something of a bohemian haunt—dark and gothic, grotty and in dire need of fumigation, like any musical rehearsal space. (The Fall also practised there, along with any number of Manchester bands planning their next gig and generally just pinning up their dreams.) More importantly, the look and feel of the place became entwined with the visual imagery of Joy Division. They spoke volumes of an era and a space and even a fashion from which the band's music flowed. Like Joy Division, it will forever be remembered in black and white.

The first anyone outside of the Manchester post-punk underground heard of Joy Division was on 20 September 1978, when they appeared on Granada TV's local show, *Granada Reports*, sandwiched between reports on motor cross and football. No prizes for guessing who got them the slot.

Their performance of 'Shadowplay' was one of the very few TV appearances the band ever made, and framed by the projected cityscape behind them, they appear both timeless and entrenched in the late 1970s. They look young, very young, and somewhat nervous. But they have a strong visual identity of their own, something that bands today would kill for. This was not a band that hired stylists, yet they gelled together seamlessly, something like four working class lads with a military mind. It was intoxicating.

The same month, Tony Wilson and Alan Erasmus formed Factory (see Chapter Two), with lofty yet humble ambitions of putting out 'art'. The label was to have an equally powerful visual identity, thanks to the guy who'd designed the posters for their club night, Peter Saville (see Chapter Eight).

In October Joy Division recorded a five-track demo session for the Genetic label (owned by the successful and much sought-after producer Martin Rushent). This session really deserves more attention, if only for the seemingly odd decisions the band made around this time. Mick Middles takes up the story.

"I think Rob [Gretton] realized that he could be a director at Factory. It's interesting, because they had no money—I mean, there was an alleged 40 grand there, but no one seems to know for sure. And the label [Genetic] had some chart success, and a good producer, rather than a mad Manc with no track record.

"Why, at that point, did they step back? No chart placings, no money, no history? Did the local TV personality [Wilson] really know what he was doing? It was an incredible thing to do. It could have been their moment. There was nothing wrong with those demos: they were very good."

So why exactly did they step back from a Genetic deal? Middles' personal theory is that Gretton saw a way forward with Factory where he could be part of the label.

"It was very astute, because if he had gone the other way, they would have tried to get rid of him straight away, all that sort of shit. So I think Rob made the right decision. They respected him for it and never looked back, but it was a *brave* decision. I think that 99 times out of 100 bands would go for the 'safe' deal, simply because there were no other deals on the table.

"Another thing is that the band were just picking up, the press were taking interest, so that would have been peaking very early."

The more hard-nosed reader might say that the plan to take the route via Wilson's Factory label wasn't in fact a successful choice. Did the increase in workload and relatively small return make for more pressure on Ian Curtis, with horrendous knock-on effects?

"In some ways you could say maybe it did backfire," Middles reflects. "Would it have been better if they'd gone?

I don't know. There would have been less pressure on Curtis. They would have had money. Maybe they made the wrong decision. But it was an odd decision. It's never really come out and I can tell you now, even Wilson doesn't know."

The first London gig for a band unfamiliar with the city is one fraught with concerns, and yet one in which so much hope is invested. Perhaps an A&R man will be in the crowd, see the band and snap them up for a tidy six-figure sum. Maybe the venue will be a grand, gold-lined den with luxurious dressing rooms and a rider for each band member.

The Hope And Anchor pub, so ingrained in the history of new guitar music, was not a gathering point for record company execs, nor was it remotely plush. It had a capacity of little more than 200 people, and the stage area lay in the very basic basement, with a more traditional pub upstairs. Joy Division's debut London gig took place there one day after Boxing Day in 1978, and only 30 people are rumored to have attended. It seems almost unbelievable now but Joy Division in London in December 1978 were not a major draw.

Indeed journalist Nick Tester, who reviewed the gig, wrote that "Joy Division's lack of an enlivening approach could be improved by an all-round sharper articulate stance and musical method. [They] could be a good band if they placed more emphasis on poise than pose." Yet within a year, Ian Curtis would be on the cover of the NME, idly smoking a cigarette, gazing into Kevin Cummins' lens.

Sadly the gig was memorable for all the wrong reasons. After the long trek in a van from Manchester (at least a four-hour journey), the band had to lug their equipment down a beer hatch to the stage, and then out again afterwards—oh the mystique of the performing arts! But a much more significant event was Ian Curtis' first epileptic fit, which occurred in the van on the return journey to Manchester.

In January 1979 Curtis was diagnosed as an epileptic. While by no means life-threatening, the condition was to have serious implications for his performances and his life with the band. More often than not, problems such as occasionally violent fits would arise from a lack of knowledge. Medication at that time was not just a pill that could be popped. The right levels of certain drugs had to be ascertained in accordance with a patient's lifestyle, and for a young man just emerging on to the rock scene while holding down a job as a civil servant and dealing with personal problems of some magnitude, rarely was anything at a constant.

In the last week of January and the second week of February 1979 Joy Division recorded their first session for the legendary DJ John Peel and the BBC's Radio 1 station. The tracks recorded at these sessions spread right across their career: 'Exercise One', 'Insight', 'She's Lost Control' and an early stab at 'Transmission'.

A John Peel session was something of a gold star for any band, especially one as absorbed by musical heritage as Joy Division. Peel had really helped many great acts, from Marc Bolan in the late 1960s right up to The Fall (who would go on to record countless sessions for the man). There was a prestige to these sessions that is evident in Joy Division's performance, and must go some way to accounting for the ease with which they run through their future single. In March the band returned to London to support The Cure at their Marquee concert, a venue rather more starry (if still heavily beer-stained) than the Hope And Anchor three months earlier.

The following month, the band walked into Stockport's Strawberry Studios for just under a week with producer Martin Hannett, to record their debut album. In June, some two months later, with a speed that must seem miraculous to anyone familiar only with today's elephantine gaps between recording and releasing a record, *Unknown Pleasures* was issued on the fledgling Factory Records.

factory records

"We'll give you everything and more"

"For a man of my years, it's easy to have that disease of
saying everything is like something that's gone before.
I know that it isn't important, but Joy Division set a blueprint
that a lot of people have followed. A lot of people have been
influenced by them, but a lot of people have taken their
ideas and run off with them, some to laughable lengths"

Marc Riley, ex-Fall bassist, Manchester

Why do people start their own record labels? Is it all about
the possibility of running your own show, in a medium you
care so much about? Or is it the last hope for people who
have realized that they can no longer entertain ideas of
becoming a musical presence themselves? Perhaps they think
that they're working for the greater good of the arts and popular culture, that they can do better than others they know.
Maybe they delude themselves into thinking the masses will
simply follow their schemes like sheep. But occasionally, perhaps, there's a talent that has to be heard, or the prospect of
a talent that needs to be coaxed from its shell, albeit with
continual funding and brown-nosing. Factory Records, by all
accounts, was all of the above.

Anthony Wilson, co-founder of Factory and a man seemingly perpetually at odds with the battle between his own

intellect and a continual tendency to undermine himself (all laced with a self-assurance that can only stem from the north of England), is all the above contradictions personified. A Cambridge graduate, he started (and still continues) his career on the small screen, first by way of the news room then by jumping from opportunity to opportunity, with the prospect of presenting new music to the masses always dangling in front of him.

"I discovered as a very young man, aged perhaps 11, that I couldn't sing. So all the work I'd done learning the folk guitar was irrelevant. I remember thinking, as a kid in Ireland, which part of my body I would trade. 'God, please, just let me be able to sing and you can have this limb!' So I couldn't sing, but I was so in love with the world of rock 'n' roll. So I found myself as a journalist, at Granada."

Already something of a 'face' on the Manchester scene, Wilson could really have chosen to start Factory with any-body, so wide were his contacts. But he chose Alan Erasmus for the main task, and designer Peter Saville to create some-thing like a visual identity.

Once a jobbing actor (he had appeared in the 1973 Mike Leigh TV play *Hard Labour*), Erasmus was now a figure on the local arts scene. A Manchester lad, he is described in Wilson's 24 *Hour Party People* as possessing "[a] gentleness [about him] that just lets Wilson get on with his stuff." And get on with things he did.

"I was making short films [for Granada]," he recalled, "and found that I could put music to them. So I found my passion and hobby had some place in my life. In 1974 I was a minor local TV newscaster at Old Trafford, so it was strange.

I remember cutting a piece with Roger Clark, the British rally driver. He was teaching me to do tailspins in the Welsh forests, and in the background I put 'LA Woman'. It was a joy at that time."

Possibilities are wonderful things, and if there's a lesson to be taken from the whirlwind story of Anthony Wilson, it's that none of them should be ignored. In Wilson's world most possibilities are seized and acted on (how many are exploited to their fullest is another matter). Generally the guiding ethos in his camp is remembered as one of 'why not?' backed up by a healthy dose of 'what's the best way to get attention from this?'—perhaps a lesson all young label bosses should learn. It may not endear you to everyone but it's the squeaky wheel that gets the grease, and Wilson was a very squeaky wheel.

"I found myself doing local arts television, and putting local bands on. That became *So It Goes*, and suddenly I found myself connected to a world I adored. Elvis Costello would smile at me before going onstage because I was the only one who liked him. Malcolm McLaren would give me a t-shirt. But it all stopped (*So It Goes was discontinued after two series*), and because I had become connected, I wanted to stay connected. And the logical way was to join my mate Erasmus in managing a band.

"[So] with A Certain Ratio and Durutti Column I became a manager for three or four years, and as Rob Gretton always used to say, I'm an utterly shite manager, an absolutely useless manager. But I found the role of record company boss more suitable to my personality."

The involvement of Gretton—justly remembered as the mentor of Joy Division and New Order—may not be quite as great as that of founders Wilson or Erasmus in the early Factory story. But his hardy nature—and the shadow he cast over Manchester's club scene—made him intrinsic to almost every aspect of the city's musical history in the 1980s.

The Russell Club in the Hulme suburb of Manchester was the first physical incarnation of the Factory presence. With Erasmus installed as 'organizer' alongside Wilson, the intention on a Friday night was to showcase bands, DJs, art, films or whatever took the fancy of the burgeoning label bosses. Its identity was created by Peter Saville's poster, all black and yellow and the first sign of the image the Hacienda club would inherit in the next decade.

Saville had approached Wilson at a gig, hoping to get some design work—remarkably this was even before the idea of Factory had been mooted. Something must have struck Wilson, because he got Saville to design the poster for the club evening of 28 May 1978. Sadly, the poster never actually saw the Russell Club walls because of a printing mix-up, but Saville has remained on the Factory panel of directors to this day.

Joy Division played their first gig at the club on 20 October 1978. It was a relatively small venue, situated tantalizingly far from the city centre (although close to one of the biggest university campuses in Europe), but the mood was one of optimism. The same was true of the new Factory concept, and more importantly, the men emerging behind it.

As a roadie and fanzine editor for Slaughter & The Dogs (his ironically titled *Manchester Rain* was based solely on the band) as well as a DJ, Rob Gretton would have experienced first-hand the lifestyle and challenges Joy Division were struggling to get a foothold in. With Gretton on board, it seemed another piece in the Factory jigsaw had slotted into place.

One of the unique things about the label was its Manchester-centric integrity—the fact that it seemed, increasingly as time wore on, to be both about and for the city. The first Factory release, the double seven-inch release *A Factory Sample* of January 1979, featured only local acts: Joy Division, The Durutti Column, Cabaret Voltaire and John Dowie. There were no contracts for the acts on the record, nor anything so complex as a royalty rate. Instead, Wilson had vowed that all bands on the label would split profits equally with it, and that they were under no pressure to stay in his stable of artists—an ideal in keeping with punk's DIY mentality.

Mick Middles believes the early Factory label was largely modelled on the way Gretton and Martin Hannett had run Rabid (see Chapter Four). "There's no doubt that Anthony Wilson watched how that label started, watched the main people involved in it—Hannett and Gretton. Gretton was really a hanger-on, but he was a massive Slaughter & The Dogs fan. He [Wilson] watched them and copied them, and took those two people, as Tosh (*Ryan, also Rabid*) would always say."

The Factory approach, combined with a suspicion of the major labels sniffing around, appealed to Joy Division. As the narrator recalls in *24 Hour Party People*, "Some guys from Warner Brothers [were] sniffing around, but it was too early for an A&R bidding war. And anyway, Barney and Rob and Steve and Pete and Ian and Tony and Alan—they were all mates."

Crispy Ambulance singer Alan Hempstall recalls the out-look of bands in Manchester towards the fledgling label. "Nobody was suspicious of Tony—he was very much 'what you see is what you get'. He knew very little about music, but in a way I think that was actually a very good thing, because he liked something because of a genuine passion rather than for a cynical reason. Anybody who operates like that, you've got to trust them really. People warned me about the whole thing, about not signing a contract. But if there's one thing Crispy Ambulance were it was realists. At the end of the day, we weren't U2. If we were to get ripped off it wouldn't have hurt that much."

With a groundswell of interest among both the press and fans, Factory built up momentum. Those northern bands on *A Factory Sample* became a kind of time capsule, representative of the early label's ethos. But from FAC 1 to FAC 10 Factory's horizons expanded. Aside from designs for menstrual egg timers (FAC 8) and varying posters, the first ten catalog numbers were allocated to bands as diverse as Joy Division, Orchestral Manoeuvres In The Dark and A Certain Ratio.

The next ten releases featured John Dowie and Durutti Column again, but also the proto-shoegazings of Section 25 ('Girls Don't Count', FAC 18), the white-boy funk of Crawling Chaos ('Sex Machine', FAC 17) and a strange attempt by producer Martin Hannett to make his own sounds ('First Aspect Of The Same Thing', one of two releases to share the FAC 14 C number).

In time this cottage industry vibe would fan out to embrace excellent, long-overlooked work from ESG (New York), 1960s 'Wimoweh' star Karl Denver (originally from

Glasgow; he would go on to work with Happy Mondays) and The Duke String Quartet (from London, on the short-lived Factory Classical offshoot).

On top of this, there was a certain zaniness to aspects like the Factory number allocation. Aside from records and VHS videos, the catalog included posters, lawsuits, dental records, model kits, badges, hair salons, bars and even a cat (resident at the Hacienda nightclub, FAC 191).

Humorous as it may be, there's something wonderfully self aware about this set up, and something quite cocksure. Instantly, one cannot be a Factory label completist, as buildings and birthday parties are hard to take home. And cats die. But in this approach, the label had, without uttering a word or writing anything down, given itself back to the city and the buildings and even the people that helped to form it. It was a seal of approval of sorts, one that Joy Division would be forever associated with, somehow on both sides of the divide.

Factory even had a continental sibling, although the exact details of the Factory Benelux label (home to remixes and different mixes of A Certain Ratio and Crispy Ambulance) remain sketchy. At the time this was the peak of cool, as if masterminded and calculated to give an international aspect to the Manchester-based indie. Anthony Wilson however, speaking to Mick Middles some 15 years later, blew the cover.

"We just received a letter one day from this guy... in Brussels. He wanted to put something out and it coincided with our first overseas Factory trip... Some people thought we were being really innovatory, by establishing a European connection so early, but all I remember is offering to give them some spare tracks. The Benelux connection was always really loose."

Yet the Factory way, somewhat aloof or even cold, was also seen by bands not on the label as something to be wary of, perhaps suspicious that it was somehow not genuine. That's the way Marc Riley, bassist in The Fall as the label started, remembers it. "The whole image was distant and standoffish. I don't mean to be disparaging, but it was very cold and very clinical. Very knowing, stylized, whereas everyone else was going out there and getting stuck in.

"They'd formulated the iconic Factory stance of people slightly not at one with the world, these angry young men. And it was fronted by this guy who, from our point of view, was a local newsreader, who was just seeing gigs every now and then."

But Riley is keen, as were many people interviewed for this book, to stress how different from such gloom Joy Division were, as people at least. "It was all so stark, it did seem quite contrived. Factory seemed to be getting all these dark young men who didn't fit in, whereas in fact, although I only bumped into Ian a few times, Bernard, Steve and Hooky are just three really great, straight fellas. Hooky is this great, ebullient, character, who is just the most approachable man in rock.

"The image they gave out, with Ian's dancing and everything, which was different to anything else, was something to behold, and Hooky's look, and the military gear, was a cold image. But they weren't, you know?"

Chris Hewitt, who co-ran the three-day Leigh Festival at which Joy Division would play, and who offered Wilson the opportunity of a Factory Day on the Sunday, is slightly less glowing in his recollections about Factory.

"I just found that the whole Factory thing was very much emperor's new clothes. I did lots of things with Tony in the early days. I worked putting sound stuff into the Hacienda right up to about 1985, we sold a lot of backline equipment to New Order, and I had a partnership in the recording studio with Hooky. But I always felt that 90 per cent of it was marketing and 10 per cent was the punters. There was a lot of hype there. And now it's blown into massive proportions.

"I always think that Tony Wilson was in a very fortunate position, in that he was a local news reporter. Therefore, as he was setting up Factory, he was able to push Joy Division, Durutti Column, A Certain Ratio into the Friday night *What's On* [*Granada TV*] spot, or the Thursday night poppy Granada production. He had inside access really. So you never know how much of it was just someone in the media perpetuating the myth."

On the subject of the Leigh Festival, Hewitt is convinced that the alleged meeting of minds it was claimed to be— between Wilson and Bill Drummond, the boss of Liverpool's Zoo Records, with both labels providing the acts—was simply not the case.

"Bill Drummond and Tony Wilson both recently claim to have organized it halfway between Manchester and Liverpool, on a bank holiday Monday. But what actually happened was that a group of youth workers in Leigh, who had several bands rehearsing at their youth club, rang me up because I'd been involved with the Deeply Vale festival, and said they were having a three-day festival, and wanted me to go down and talk about the stage, the lights, look at the site, and help them out with it.

"So I had a look, gave them a price, and then they were talking about bands. So I suggested Supercharge for the Saturday night, because they were a good, rabble-rousing, group with a fantastic brass section, a good festival band to dance to. And I suggested that they got in touch with Tony Wilson, to get some Factory bands on for one of the days. So it was a three-day event, but Factory were only providing bands for the third day.

"Of course, history has now been rewritten, and it's as if Tony Wilson and Bill Drummond had this idea to put on a Factory meets Zoo half-way gig, when they didn't at all. It was bollocks—they were asked to provide bands. And the poster, FAC 15: The Leigh Festival, or whatever, I never saw one of those in my life and I was at the festival every day and all round Leigh. (*The festival poster was designed by Peter Saville, in a run of just 300, to promote the event.*) It was probably one of those great things Peter Saville did and it arrived three weeks afterwards.

"And of course, no one came to the Leigh Festival. That great bill of Joy Division, A Certain Ratio, Echo & The Bunnymen, Teardrop Explodes, OMD… and there were about 20 people in the audience. On the Joy Division day, that was probably about the most, 20 or 30 people."

Nevertheless, Joy Division would come to embody a kind of 'first phase' for Factory—in no small part thanks to the visual identity provided by Saville but also because of the mood of their era. Away from the music, the spirit of Joy Division in the late 1970s was as reflective as that of anyone living in the aftermath of punk. The people at Factory, friends of course, were all experiencing, experimenting with and trying to start exactly the same things. Now neatly sealed in their one-album-in-a-lifespan bubble, with no possibility of a return, Joy Division have come to symbolize the young label. New Order, the label's heyday and scrappy demise that followed, can never touch this.

Anthony Wilson, of course, is proud of what he did, and continues with the label in its fourth guise, promoting records by street-based rap collectives and his ever-reliable Vini Reilly/Durutti Column. But the significance of having a band like Joy Division on the label does not escape him.

"Everybody should start a label. Except the thing is, the rule is to only start it when you see an artist who is wonderful. I couldn't imagine running a label if all your acts are shite. It's a wonderful experience, watching your group grow. There's absolutely nothing like it.

"But you must be absolutely committed and utterly shocked that a record hasn't sold more, angry and defensive, hysterical even. Commitment is what it's all about."

But what is the man's secret? Is he just a chancer? The wanker he willed himself to be portrayed as in 24 *Hour Party People*? Or simply very lucky?

"I don't recognize my own talent. I am quite good at spotting art. I have a talent for it. That is a real talent, but my only one. The prime example of that isn't Joy Division or New Order or the Mondays and it's not the bands I put on television. It's the bands I *didn't* put on TV.

"It's a little arrogant, but the 73 bands I put on telly for the first time, I was right about. But what people don't remember are the 473 bands I turned down. I was right about all of them as well. Including The Boomtown Rats.

"If I go to a basement gig in Manchester or New York, and see a band and then don't do anything with them, and then they make [a record like] 'Love Will Tear Us Apart' three years later, I'd slit my throat. I'd retire. It would be over. Today, at the age of 55, I am as passionate and as involved as ever. I'm useless at anything else."

What it really comes down to is the fact that Wilson was there, and he actually acted upon his ideas. Others might have sensed a buzz around the young Joy Division or even Warsaw before them, but Wilson was the man who actually formed the label and put their records out. Wilson is wildly philosophical on the matter, but wonderfully modest to boot.

"One thing I do have is enthusiasm, and that's useful for musicians. I realized that I have a very British relationship with my musicians. You're friends with your musicians but your real relationship is with the manager, whereas in Europe the bosses of the labels have a *personal* relationship with the musicians. But with Joy Division, as well as being their mates, you were also passionately committed to their genius. And if they hear you saying, 'You are fucking great,' that's great. If you can promote that self-belief, that sense of self, then that's all the better. I believed in them for them. Which was of some value."

punk and the tendrils

"Turned on to a knife-edged view"

"I think all bands back then were atrocious live.
But that was part and parcel of the scene.
Mistakes, poor sound, all of those things"

Chris Hewitt, Deeply Vale festival organizer, Mere

To understand the influence of the emerging post-punk scene
on Warsaw and Joy Division, the effects of punk itself have
to be considered. The punk scene was incendiary wherever it
arose. Manchester gave us Buzzcocks (and later Magazine),
and we have already touched on their influence on Ian
Curtis. But were Devoto, Shelley *et al* just the tip of the ice-
berg when it came to the Manchester punk scene? Were
there a million bands in the city that the public never got to
hear about? In short, what kind of local scene did Joy
Division sprout from?

According to Mick Middles, it was one of pomp and
overly complicated musicianship—the world of prog rock.
"[The Electric Circus] was actually a hippy or progressive
rock venue. They [the locals] regarded it quite preciously
really. And then punk came along...

"I remember one night The Enid (*pseudo-classical ultra-
hippies*) were supposed to be playing, as they used to a lot,
but they switched the bill to The Dammed at the last

minute. All these Enid fans were there—this was November 1976—and The Dammed walked on stage..."

Around this time Ian Curtis would definitely have been attending the Circus, as it was the real heart of the city's live music scene. While the idea that Curtis might have been rebelling against any particular style of music in his early years is rarely debated, surely the pomp and lengthy, instrumental, music of bands like The Enid would make him reach for his Krautrock, or his glam, or even reggae records? Or was Curtis once a prog rock fan?

"The strange thing was," says Middles, "most of those prog rock fans became punks—seemingly without transition. Then it [the Electric Circus] became a punk venue. The same people with shorter hair. The Dammed finished their set with 'New Rose', and at the end there was this massive chorus from the crowd of 'Shit! Shit! Shit!'. Then, three minutes later, the same people were all dancing around to Black Sabbath's 'Paranoid' and I couldn't help thinking they sounded the same. But that was the center, not the Lesser Free Trade Hall thing. The Circus was the center of it all really."

So the punk movement in Manchester found a venue it could call its own. But there were many other contenders springing up, all looking for bands to play, and all seemingly as grotty and unsuitable as the next. Some even had their own set of hazards, as Middles remembers...

"The Band On The Wall was like a London pub venue. It was an old jazz club, but it just looked like a London pub. So the Buzzcocks would play there, and the Rants bar, which was like a meeting place for all the punks. And that was next to Fifi Lemars, which was a riotous, stag-night type place. It used to get raided by these teddy boys, so suddenly there were teds to fight the punks, but there weren't teds before the punks, and there weren't teds afterwards. I don't know where they came from.

"I remember going to a Slaughter & The Dogs gig in Salford, and there were about 100 of them, and they smashed all the windows. They were men in their thirties. Maybe they wanted to reclaim their rock 'n' roll heritage or something. After a couple of months they vanished. To this day I've no idea where they came from or where they went! Or why they did it..."

Could the Sex Pistols' gig at the Lesser Free Trade Hall really have been the only catalyst for Buzzcocks to start their own New Hormones label and record their debut, just 27 days after the Pistols' swearing outrage on Bill Grundy's *Today* show? Surely, rivalry and punk being as they were, the rise of acts like Buzzcocks was a defiant declaration that the north of England could make music as vital and exciting as the south? Did the punks of Manchester not in fact dislike and want to react against the stylized southerners?

Mick Middles: "I think the difference was that London was always perceived as being more posey. You had Vivienne Westwood clothes, which we never, ever had up here. No one had money. I mean, there weren't punks up here: you just had to wear drainpipe trousers and that was it—basically, not have long hair. That was enough to make a statement and get attacked on buses.

"Some of the London punks came up to the Free Trade Hall, and some came up with Chelsea when they played at the Circus, Mark Perry or whoever, with the leather trousers, and they didn't quite mix. Actually, at the Lesser Free Trade Hall gig there was quite a bit of trouble between the London people and the Manchester people. It's not been reported, and it got quite heavy."

So the prevailing memory of punk gigs in Manchester might be one of violence, and of dank, dark, sweaty, rooms. Was there competition between The Fall and Joy Division? Was there a rivalry as a shift in the tides meant the music of choice for discerning listeners moved from simple 1-2-3 of punk to more cerebral acts like Talking Heads, the rockabilly-infused political stance of The Clash or the electronic pioneering work of Germany's Kraftwerk? Marc Riley recalls the scene.

"When I first met them I was in the band I was in before I was in The Fall. Buzzcocks had taken off, Magazine were looming large (*Howard Devoto had left Buzzcocks to form Magazine in February 1977*), and The Fall were established, to an extent. Warsaw were also established to an extent, but The Fall were always just nudging ahead a little bit. The Fall went to London first, The Fall got a deal first, The Fall got a good review first...

"I was in a band called The Sirens (*with Steve Hanley and Craig Scanlon, who both joined The Fall about a year after Riley*). We used to rehearse at T.J. Davidsons, on Little Peter Street, so we used to see them [Warsaw] a lot, and we knew them a little bit. We'd say hello. They were a gigging band, and we were just awful—we only played one gig. We were more like Buzzcocks than anything, really fast Buzzcocks.

"But then the bass player got kicked out of The Fall, and I went for the job. All of a sudden I went from this position of looking up to Warsaw, who had probably become Joy Division by this point, admiring that they were a proper working band with a record out, [to being] in The Fall and slightly, only ever so slightly, looking down on them. We just managed to do everything just before them, you know?"

The agitation of punk may have passed by the likes of Warsaw and The Fall, perhaps replaced by a more studious approach to music—even the famous Manchester miserablism. Riley agrees, although he also recalls a certain low-key tension between the bands.

"There was a famous gig at Bowdon Vale, which is quite a middle-class suburb just outside Altrincham, a well-to-do area. They [Joy Division] played two shows at the Bowdon Vale Youth Club, and once The Sirens had split up, the other members formed a band called Staff 9, and they were supporting Joy Division. I went along as Staff 9's roadie. So I walked in carrying amps, and Joy Division were on the stage sound-checking, and they stopped half way through a song and Hooky started playing a Fall song. Being a miserable git at the time, I thought he was taking the mickey, but he probably wasn't. He was probably just being friendly. But I'd already been indoctrinated in the miserablist attitude, after just being in the band [The Fall] for a few months."

The music press of the post-punk era also inadvertently contributed to this budding local rivalry.

"Dave McCullough, from *Sounds*, reviewed *Live At The Witch Trials* [*The Fall's debut album in 1979*] and gave it five stars and said it was the best debut album since The Clash's debut. We did pretty well, and a lot of press came through, so Joy Division slipped a little bit. Then Dave McCullough, again I think, got hold of *Unknown Pleasures*, and gave that an equally brilliant review. And then [things took] off."

But rather than hold either group back, it seemed the competition, combined with the city finding its musical feet and beginning to compete with London, actually helped raise awareness of what was on offer. The punk scene, it seemed, had achieved its mission statement of 'doing it yourself'. Nowhere was this more evident than in the number of venues that were fast becoming accessible to the growing Manc-punk army. (The exception, ironically, was the Lesser Free Trade Hall, as Mick Middles recalls: "There were never any other gigs there. Devoto and Shelley [Buzzcocks] must've got it cheap.")

Pips nightclub, now sadly a salon across the square from the ultra modern Urbis museum, was home to the first Joy Division gig after the name change from Warsaw. The punks in the city seemed to make it their second home.

"In the early 1970s it was the Nice & Easy," Middles recalls fondly, "which was probably the best nightclub in Manchester. Then Pips disco used to have the Roxy Rooms, where all the Bowie freaks used to go. You used to go there to hear The Stooges and all that stuff, which was part of the Manchester punk scene as well. It lasted until bands like Dexy's [Midnight Runners] played there.

"But it was important, because it was the only place you could go where you could hear The Stooges or The New York Dolls—everywhere else was like disco. [It] was the most posey place, and the punk scene in Manchester was married to that side of it, the glam side. It's like everywhere else—the kids who listened to T.Rex became punks."

Joy Division made headway away from Manchester too, their slowly growing fanbase at out-of-town gigs (such as York or Canterbury) bolstered by any number of local punks starved of bands and rabid for the music they had heard and read so much about. Further London gigs followed, first as support to acts such as The Cure, but later in the band's own right. The decision to support Buzzcocks on a whole tour not only took Joy Division countrywide to venues they would otherwise have not seen, but also acted as a kind of stamp of approval.

The fact that Joy Division were playing well made such first impressions all the more significant. More frequent gigging had honed their skills, but the band also toughened up as people—perhaps demonstrated by a conquering of pre-gig nerves or an ability to deal with wayward fans such as hardcore punks eager to get the support act off stage so the main band could come on.

Behind the scenes, away from the concerts and the press coverage, a network of record labels was forming. Many of these labels were short-lived but Factory was building up a head of steam, averaging one release a month in its first year (even if some of these 'releases' were not actually records). In 1979 the city of Manchester, having been woken up by the supernova of punk, was sitting up and listening. Now those listeners were taking stock, making their own noises and planning their own strategies.

the question of martin hannett

"I've been waiting for a guide to come"

"I've actually listened to Unknown Pleasures a lot over the last few years and it amazes me how astonishing the songs still sound. Twenty-five years is a long time, but every song still sounds timeless and astonishingly modern"

Peter Saville, designer, Manchester

Recollections of the role of producer Martin Hannett in the rapidly evolving sound of Joy Division are divided straight down the middle. There are those who believe that his work in the studio, often volatile but usually productive at some point, was a matter of chance—that the musicians brought the only essential ingredient into the room. The other side of the coin shows a man with a deep love of many styles of music, one who truly *saw* sound, and more importantly, saw the sound he wanted the bands he was working with to achieve.

Born in Manchester in 1950, Hannett became involved in any number of aspects of the city's music scene at a young age, even more so after dropping out of a degree course in chemistry at the Polytechnic. With Tosh Ryan and Rob Gretton, he was one of three managing directors of the Rabid label, which had been largely set up to release records by

Gretton's pet love, punk band Slaughter & The Dogs. Far from being a simple fan project, however, Rabid went on to release records by such Manchester luminaries as Ed Banger, Chris Sievey (The Freshies), John Cooper Clarke and the chart-bothering Jilted John. Hannett would have baulked at being seen as its in-house producer, but his work with Slaughter & The Dogs—particularly their scorching debut 'Cranked Up Really High'—left a mini-legacy strong enough for Ian Brown to seek him out in the late 1980s, to work on the first version of The Stone Roses' single, 'Elephant Stone.'

"[He] was the first producer we worked with. He had produced our favorite single, 'Cranked Up Really High' by Slaughter & The Dogs, and in Manchester, you either liked Buzzcocks or Slaughter & The Dogs. So that's why we worked with Martin. It was an amazing experience to work with a guy like that."

As well as writing for the *New Manchester Review*, Hannett ran a kind of musical smorgasbord called Music Force in Wythenshawe, on the outskirts of the city. What exactly the company did remains unclear; suffice it to say the position provided Hannett with enough contacts to offer groups from the area 'packages' of help, be it through promoting gigs, arranging gigs or just helping with posters.

As Mick Middles remembers: "They [Music Force] go back to 1971 and The Squat. Their idea was to be gig promoters who were independent of London, who controlled everything. So they were promoting gigs, and there were bands like The Albertos that were part of it all, but then it sort of split, and in 1976, 1977 Hannett was running the gig side of things from an office above the *New Manchester Review*. Tosh [*Ryan, his business partner*] had started the poster business, which became a big underground business. Out of it all came Slaughter & The Dogs and the Rabid label, and Absurd later on.

"So they were into a bit of everything really. It was all a bit sort of unofficial, a bit dodgy, but I guess it's kind of romantic in its own way. With 25 years distance."

Indeed romance plays a large part in any remembrance of Martin Hannett. Quite aside from his work in the studio, he is described at various points as 'difficult', 'eccentric' or at worst, 'a junkie'. In the film 24 *Hour Party People* his character is seen to bark at Stephen Morris over a studio intercom system. Nothing special there, you might think—until the camera reveals that the drum kit is being played on the roof of the studio, and is not even being recorded.

Stories like this litter the greater part of any memory of Hannett. Middles recalls that "he literally had a nuts and bolts approach. There's that story about dismantling the drum kit, which is a little overdone but it was true. That's what he did, that sort of Germanic beat. Maybe it was luck. People say it's genius, I don't know."

Stephen Morris expanded on the legendary drum tale when speaking to press in 2005. "I thought the drums would only take as long as the song is to record but no, no... that wasn't it at all. Martin wanted everything recorded separately, so we started with just the bass drum—literally just me and the bass drum. Then the snare and then the hi-hat again, all completely separate. He wanted to get the sounds as isolated as possible but it didn't feel natural at all for me to play the songs like that. I can understand what he wanted, with the benefit of hindsight, but at the time I couldn't see the point of it."

What can we surmise from these stories, these tales of a mad man forever chasing a sound in his head that he might never attain? Stories of a band just agreeing with everything he said so as to get home at a reasonable hour. What exactly did Martin Hannett do in the studio?

"Well, it was a little tricky," says Ian Brown, "because he was really, really deep in to class As (*hard drugs*). He had a driver, and every half an hour he'd be getting someone to drive him off to pick something up. He'd spend a couple of hours under the desk cross-legged, things like that. Then he'd put his old Joy Division quarter-inches (*tapes*) on, to remind himself how to do it. The funniest thing was that he was sat at the mixing desk one day, and he had this great big belly, and he was pushing the dials forward with his belly. The engineer came over to fix it, and he said, 'No, leave that—that's the Martin Hannett curve, the curved sound of Martin Hannett, leave it…'

"The first thing we did was called 'So Young' and it was so extreme it made the [Jesus &] Mary Chain sound like Abba. It was so trebly and feedback-y that [*Stone Roses' drummer*] Reni's nose exploded when we played it in the car. There was blood all over. It was so extreme. We should have gone with that version, but we didn't. We toned it down and did another one."

Brown's recollection illustrates perfectly the three strands to Hannett's troubled life. First, there was his problem with drugs that plagued him until (and led to) his death in 1991. Second, there were his odd ways of working, his seemingly pointless routines and half-baked ideas (could a sound really be any good if the levels were decided by the shape of his beer belly?). But perhaps most heartbreakingly, there's the point where Hannett has to listen back to Joy Division tapes, some six or seven years after the event, to motivate himself to work. Just why were those tapes so good?

Part of the answer lies in Hannett's introduction of synthesizers to the Joy Division sound, which turned them into a completely different beast from the maudlin, half-good, half-bad, punk band they were before they met him.

"You have to listen to it. The snare sound that he gave Joy Division was a lot thinner," recalls Crispy Ambulance's Alan Hempstall. "But he had to, I guess, because there's quite a lot of space in there. And I think that's what Martin was taking advantage of. I don't think our snare sound would have worked with something like, say, 'Disorder'—it just has to be clipped, clicky-clacky, kind of sound, rather than a popping, numb, sound."

Chris Hewitt, who put on the Leigh Festival at which Joy Division played, is fulsome in his praise of Hannett. "I think Martin Hannett is the secret of Joy Division. Ian had some great ideas for lyrics—perhaps they were about his personal torture, his life, his marriage, his upbringing. But Martin took what was basically a gloomy punk band and added all sorts of experimental sound, the early synths and all sorts of strange and wonderful effects, and created that electronic thing with them."

That view is endorsed by Middles, but he also highlights a change in drumming styles. "Hannett was the link really that changed everything. There were two Russell Club Factory gigs, I think within about three weeks, and you had the old Joy Division and the new Joy Division. The first gig was very much like, 'OK, they're getting better' but there was still something muddy about them. It was the rock drumming basically. But the next time there was this sharp, disco type of drumming, and that must have been where Hannett came in."

Comparing Warsaw demos to the tracks on the *Unknown Pleasures* album, you can hear Middles' point. A track such as 'Shadowplay', sludgy and a touch labored in its earliest incarnation, is freed by Morris' furiously paced drumming after the Hannett touch. But the question that remains: did Hannett actually instruct the band to play in this new manner, or did the continual practising and gigging lead the band to find their own sound?

Alan Hempstall is sceptical that Hannett would have done anything more than harness the emerging sound the band were creating live. "Martin was ultimately a studio animal—the guy was a producer. What you've got to remember is, with any band, there is a live aspect, and the live aspect with Joy Division was quite phenomenal. Occasionally you had gigs where Ian might have been a bit ill, and if he was ill his voice tended to weaken, and I think that's evident on some live recordings. You can tell when Ian's poorly—some of those gigs are painful to hear—he's not on full song. But when he *was*, the band were always there, the band were strong."

This is a point worth remembering. While it is true that Joy Division had a very short life as a performing entity, what they achieved technically within that time remains very impressive. Their sound, therefore, may well have just evolved through the rigors of being a band, rather than through tweaking techniques in the studio, as it is often perceived.

"I think you can hear it in old interviews from the period—that post-punk period. They were listening to The Pop Group, Red Krayola, or whatever," Middles recalls, "so their heads were practically three months ahead of where they were physically. They were pulling ahead of their peers and the stuff they were playing was moving very fast—almost, weirdly, as if they had to get this new stuff in before something bad happened. Looking back you can see it, because from Warsaw to *Closer*, all they had was a very dodgy, sub-Banshees band that turned into the band that recorded *Closer*—astonishing."

The odd ways of working that The Stone Roses experienced with Hannett seem to have had an influence even when *Unknown Pleasures* was gestating. As Stephen Morris remembered in 2005: "His dialogs were always so vague. One time I was moonlighting by playing drums on a John Cooper Clarke album that Martin was producing at the same time as *Unknown Pleasures*. I did about three takes of one track and there was silence from the control room. Eventually he would say 'Yeah it's OK—do it again but this time, make it a bit more... cocktail party.' I just humored him."

Probably the closest to understanding what Hannett was trying to achieve, particularly in those early days, was offered by Tony Wilson, speaking to *Record Collector* magazine in 2005. "Martin explained to me what he was trying to do with his production. As I understand it, every time you hear a sound, you don't know it but your brain is telling you where you are and where the sound is coming from according to the amount of reverb, delay and so on. It creates an imaginary room. That's what you get on those modern hi-fis where you can press buttons to make it sound like a concert hall or a live gig or whatever. What the great producers like Martin do is create a different room for every *mood*."

Cruelly, we will never know what Joy Division after Hannett would have sounded like, so the precise nature of this enigmatic figure's contribution to their music may never be definitively dissected for posterity.

some notes on the equipment used
"Me in my own world"

Guitars

Peter Hook and Bernard Sumner probably stumbled upon the Shergold brand of guitars because of affordability, rather than through any artistic choice or desire to emulate someone else. Hook, however, still uses his six-string bass from that firm today, and was somewhat involved in the company relaunch in 1991 (it had gone bankrupt in 1981 and sadly met the same fate second time around).

"Shergold was a British brand that appeared in 1960," says *Total Guitar*'s Henry Yates. "[It was] established by two former employees of Burns (*another UK company*) and mainly made guitars and parts for other firms until 1976. After this point, it mass-produced guitars in its own right."

Though much of the firm's output was good quality, it was somewhat unfashionable. Yates again: "Shergold guitars had flashy finishes—apple green, for instance—and didn't just ape the US models—they used an unusual hardwood called obechi, but they weren't especially cool. Their most successful model was the Masquerader. It's got two humbucking pick-ups—giving the guitar a thicker, fatter, tone that's more prone to distorting than, say, a Fender Stratocaster—and a naff black plastic 'badge' over the bridge, which most people removed."

It was the Shergold Custom Masquerader that Sumner would use while in Joy Division, alongside Gibson and Gibson copy models. The original 1974 advertisement for it recommended a retail price of £170.29 and these days the price remains comparatively low, even allowing for inflation and desirability (it received glowing endorsements from the likes of Genesis' Mike Rutherford). Where Sumner got the model with the distinctive ribbed headstock and double scratchplate isn't known, but the guitar is a black version of the six-string he used on the *Something Else* programme, with white DiMarzio pick-ups and a Fender tremolo arm added.

In 1977, at the time of Warsaw, Sumner was also using a copy of the iconic Gibson SG. He would move on to a legitimate brand-name version of the guitar later.

Finally, Sumner's white Vox 'Teardrop' was similar in scale to the Phantom and is a stylish joy to behold. In visual terms, it shouldn't work in the confines of a band like Joy Division, but there is something wonderfully childlike about Sumner strumming away at the rounded body that works so well.

Yates: "The Mk IV Teardrop appeared in 1963 and it's still an icon of that decade. It has single-coil pickups (*giving a bright, more metallic sound that is typical of Joy Division*) and a Bigsby tremolo (*for bending notes*). You can get US-built reissues these days, but one imagines Joy Division had an original."

Peter Hook would also use the Shergold brand, playing his trademark six-string Marathon bass. The model is famous in guitar circles for its synth-inspired sound, which the bassist would use to more devastating effect on later, more club-orientated, tracks like New Order's 'Blue Monday'.

At the time of recording *Unknown Pleasures*, however, Hook would most probably have used his comparatively cheap copy of the Gibson EBO bass, which he had bought from Mazel's Music Shop in Manchester at some point after the Lesser Free Trade Hall Pistols gig in 1976. Yates comments: "The Gibson EBO has twin 'horn'-like cutaways and a single humbucking pickup (*for thick, thudding tones*)."

Other contenders for recordings of the time included another copy, made by Hondo in the style of a Rickenbacker bass, and one of the more traditional Yamaha BB 1200s. The latter is simplicity itself—a bass that allows playing high up the neck, something that lends itself well to Hook's low-slung style of playing. This model is also noted for its suitability for soloing.

The more workhorse members of Hook's bass guitar artillery were the Yamaha BB 1200 and the Shergold Marathon. They were perhaps not as important or easily recognizable as their other instruments, but they were all vital to the sound of the band. Yates again: "The Yamaha is a highly regarded four-string Japanese bass, and the Shergold in this section is a six-string [as opposed to the traditional four]."

When it comes to effects, it is usually taken as read that Hook only really used one pedal—the Electro Harmonix Clone Theory chorus/vibrato. In recent years effects-laden grunge artists like Dinosaur Jnr have exploited the pedal, and it's easy to hear why. Where other effects pedals 'max-out' or distort, the Clone Theory is said to be just beginning. Many years before the pedal was snapped up by youngsters desperate to sound like Nirvana's Kurt Cobain, Hook had discovered its almost submerged sound, using its bubbly style in creating a sound of his own. The vibrato on the pedal is often compared to the wavering qualities of guitar music from the late 1950s and early 1960s.

Ian Curtis' guitar, the Vox Phantom IV Special, is perhaps more famous for the way it looked than the sound it made. It was a rather strange guitar for a band of the punk era to pick up on. Henry Yates: 'The standard Vox Phantom was introduced in 1961. It's got a trapezoid-shaped body—likened by many to a coffin—and single-coil pickups, giving snappier, more trebly tones. This guitar was kind of unfashionable in the 1970s, and cheap as a result.'

Anyone who likes to read the macabre into all matters Curtis might conclude it was chosen for its coffin-like shape, but its real significance lies in its trebly sound, particularly in Joy Division's live performances—it's the perfect counterbalance to Peter Hook's bowel-loosening bass. The influence of The Velvet Underground's Sterling Morrison should not be downplayed either.

Synthesizers and keyboards

The star of Joy Division's keyboard collection would have undoubtedly been the ARP Omni-2 synthesizer, which would come further into the limelight on the *Closer* album. Still revered today (although perhaps more for its influence on mid-to-late-1980s club music than Joy Division's work), it was the improved version of the company's Onmi model. It had a built-in bass synthesizer, and was practically three instruments in one smooth, black, box. Primarily a string section, it also offered a polyphonic keyboard and a separate bass synth. It was ARP's best selling model, and can also be heard on records by such disparate artists as ELO, War, Stevie Wonder and Supertramp.

Also used: ARP Solina String Ensemble, Powertran Transcendent 2000, ETI, Melodian.

Selected Effects: Melos echo, MXR 10-band graphic equalizer, chorus flanger, Altair PW-5 power attenuator.

Drums

It remains unclear exactly which drum kit Stephen Morris used in Joy Division's lifetime, if indeed he settled on one at all in the punk era. It is known he liked the Rogers concert kit, along with a whole rack of drum machines including the Simmonds twin-channel synthesizer, the Synare three-drum synthesizer, the Musicaid Claptrap and Boss DR55 drum machine at different points. By the time of New Order, Morris was reported to be receiving items of new equipment from manufacturers, all hoping their kit would be used on a record, so influential had his sound become.

track by track: before unknown pleasures

"All you judges beware"

"I got into Joy Division years ago. I guess I was struggling emotionally to cope with the pressures of life, and they simply struck a chord. The darkness and the unashamed bleakness somehow gave me hope. Most people hear them as really depressing, but they help me to transcend the bullshit of the everyday. They captured everything I was thinking and feeling, and not necessarily the lyrics. Initially it was just about the sound and the production, and that haunting voice. It excites me in a way that no other music has. It's a gut reaction. There are moments when I hear something new, a bassline, a lyric, and it takes my breath away. The pure beauty astounds me"

Jessica Penfold, 23, London (who has four of the sound waves from the Unknown Pleasures *cover tattooed on her back)*

Recordings referred to in the following chapters (in order of earliest official release):

Short Circuit 2 (Virgin, VCL 5003, 10/77)
Features: 'At A Later Date'

An Ideal For Living (Enigma, PSS 139, 6/78)
Tracklisting: 'Warsaw' / 'No Love Lost' / 'Leaders Of Men' /
'Failures'

A Factory Sample (Factory, FAC 2, 12/78)
Features: 'Digital' and 'Glass'

Unknown Pleasures (Factory, FACT 10, 6/79)
Tracklisting: 'Disorder' / 'Day Of The Lords' / 'Candidate' /
'Insight' / 'New Dawn Fades' / 'She's Lost Control' /
'Shadowplay' / 'Wilderness' / 'Interzone' / 'I Remember
Nothing'

Earcom 2 (Fast Product, FAST 9B, 10/79)
Features: 'Autosuggestion' and 'From Safety To Where…?'

'Transmission' / 'Novelty' (Factory, FAC 13, 10/79)

'Atmosphere' / 'She's Lost Control' (Factory, FACUS 2, 9/80)

Still (Factory, FACT 40, 10/81)
Tracklisting: 'Exercise One' / 'Ice Age' / 'The Sound Of
Music' / 'Glass' / 'The Only Mistake' / 'Walked In Line' /
'The Kill' / 'Something Must Break' / 'Dead Souls' / 'Sister
Ray' / 'Ceremony' (live) / 'Shadowplay' (live) / 'Means To An
End' (live) / 'Passover' (live) / 'New Dawn Fades' (live) /
'Transmission' (live) / 'Disorder' (live) / 'Isolation' (live) /
'Decades' (live) / 'Digital' (live)

Permanent (London, 3984282212, 8/85)
Tracklisting: 'Love Will Tear Us Apart' / 'Transmission' / 'She's Lost Control' / 'Shadowplay' / 'Day Of The Lords' / 'Isolation' / 'Passover' / 'Heart And Soul' / 'Twenty Four Hours' / 'These Days' / 'Novelty' / 'Dead Souls' / 'The Only Mistake' / 'Something Must Break' / 'Atmosphere' / 'Love Will Tear Us Apart' (Permanent Mix)

Peel Sessions EP (Strange Fruit, SFPS 013, 1986)
Tracklisting: 'Exercise One' / 'Insight' / 'She's Lost Control' / 'Transmission'

Substance (Factory, FACT 250, 1988)
'Warsaw' / 'Leaders Of Men' / 'Digital' / 'Autosuggestion' / 'Transmission' / 'She's Lost Control' / 'Incubation' / 'Dead Souls' / 'Atmosphere' / 'Love Will Tear Us Apart' / 'No Love Lost' / 'Failures' / 'Glass' / 'From Safety To Where…?' / 'Novelty' / 'Komakino' / 'These Days'

'Atmosphere' / 'Transmission' / 'Love Will Tear Us Apart' (Factory, FACD 213, 6/88)

Warsaw (Movieplay Gold, MPG 74034, 1994)
Tracklisting: 'Drawback' / 'Leaders Of Men' / 'They Walked In Line' / 'Failures' / 'Novelty' / 'No Love Lost' / 'Transmission' / 'Living In The Ice Age' / 'Interzone' / 'Warsaw' / 'Shadowplay' / 'As You Said' / 'Inside The Line' / 'Gutz' / 'At A Later Date' / 'Kill' / 'You're No Good For Me'

Heart And Soul (London, 828968-2, 1997)
This 4-CD set purports to contain the entirety of Joy
Division's recorded output, although certain session tracks
are omitted.

Preston 28 February 1980 (NMC, FACD 2.60, 1999)
Tracklisting (all recorded live): 'Incubation' / 'Wilderness' /
'Twenty Four Hours' / 'The Eternal' / 'Heart And Soul' /
'Shadowplay' / 'Transmission' / 'Disorder' / 'Warsaw' /
'Colony' / 'Interzone' / 'She's Lost Control'

The Complete BBC Recordings (Strange Fruit, SFRSCD
094, 6/00)
Tracklisting: 'Exercise One' / 'Insight' / 'She's Lost Control' /
'Transmission' / 'Love Will Tear Us Apart' / 'Twenty Four
Hours' / 'Colony' / 'Sound Of Music' / 'Transmission' / 'She's
Lost Control'

Les Bains Douches 18 December 1979 (NMC, FACD
2.61, 2001)
Tracklisting (all recorded live): 'Disorder' / 'Love Will Tear Us
Apart' / 'Insight' / 'Shadowplay' / 'Transmission' / 'Day Of The
Lords' / 'Twenty Four Hours' / 'These Days' / 'A Means To An
End' / 'Passover' / 'New Dawn Fades' / 'Atrocity Exhibition' /
'Digital' / 'Dead Souls' / 'Autosuggestion' / 'Atmosphere'

Before And After: The BBC Sessions (Fuel, SFRSCD 094,
7/02)
Features: same tracks as The Complete BBC Recordings,
with extra New Order disc.

Refractured (Alchemy, no catalogue number, 1/04)
Tracklisting (all recorded live): the complete Les Bains
Douches set and the complete Preston set.

From here onwards, releases are discussed in order of
recording:

Warsaw Demo Sessions
Recorded: 18/7/77, Pennine Sound Studios, Oldham
Produced by: Warsaw
All available on: *Warsaw*

If nothing else, the earliest Warsaw sessions serve as proof that
practise makes perfect when it comes to playing in a band.
While not as pedestrian or run-through as some critics would
have you believe, these embryonic tracks come across as being
more at home in the live arena. While there is little to distin-
guish the songs from the chanting punk of the day, a Joy
Division fan can still hear in these skeletal, crudely produced
demos the first signs of a unique talent seeping through.

At A Later Date
Also recorded: 29/10/77, Electric Circus Club, Manchester
Also available on: *Short Circuit 2*

Listening to 'At A Later Date' is something of a trial. The
song relies too heavily on the barrack room shout, popular-
ized by the likes of Sham 69. Steve Brotherdale's drums,
though competent, lack the mechanical shimmer that

Stephen Morris would produce, and it is only when Ian Curtis' voice cracks, say, at the end of a verse, that we briefly feel any sense of real emotion from him.

It doesn't help that the lyrics are comparatively trite. Every rhyme sounds forced, and many of the verses are filled to the brim with clumsily rhythmic syllables. There is cod philosophy ("Why are we all here?") and a hint of anti-consumerism ("Can't buy everything, that's true"), but on the whole it is evident that Curtis is still finding his poetic feet, while conforming with the fashionable sense of alienation and anti-establishment ideals of the era.

On a more positive note, Peter Hook plays a consistent and innovative bassline, although somewhat at odds with the other instruments (perhaps as a result of being so high in the mix), and there is something about Sumner's simple yet glacial guitar line that rewards repeated listens.

The live recording from the Electric Circus on *Short Circuit* 2 has an instrumental balance much more suited to the song, with only Curtis' vocals lacking punch. However, his baritone is kept in check, and a clear indication begins to emerge as to where his most effective style might lie—the desperate howl at the top end of his register. Primarily though, this version is most notable for the life which the metronomic Morris breathes into it with his concise yet frenzied drumming.

Gutz

Commencing with the lowest Peter Hook bassline ever caught on tape and clocking in at less than two minutes, the punchy, throbbing, 'Gutz' (formerly 'Gutz For Garters') sounds the most unlike Joy Division of any Warsaw material.

Heavily in debt to the Sex Pistols, the track practically folds in on itself in the rush to make a crowd pogo. From the opening cry of "Warsaw!" to the pained exclamation of "No comment, copycat!" at the close, 'Gutz' is a hate song in the most traditional punk sense.

What the listener mainly gets from 'Gutz' is a sense of urgency. Ability is outrun by ambition, and each member of the band seems to over-compensate for his inadequacies by playing up to his role. Curtis is deep of voice and screams when a subtle intonation, as he would learn, would be much more effective. Hook pounds the bass, adding notes and musical syllables at every opportunity, and Sumner seems intent on soloing throughout the whole song. These were different times indeed.

Inside The Line

'Inside The Line' slows the pace. From the simple chord structure between each verse to the novel, phased, bass run around the 1:20 mark that returns 25 seconds from the end, the song offers a brief insight into the sonic experimentation which would be exploited by Martin Hannett's production the following year.

More significant, though, are Curtis' lyrics. By far the best these sessions provided, perhaps as a direct consequence of a slower pace, they are given the space they need to have effect. A distinctive vocal style has still to be discovered, but lines like "Suffocation comes too easy, I just want some time to breathe" or "Crowded in a room for one, darkness when the lights are on" stand up far better than much of the output from this time. With them Curtis creates a sense of paranoia and claustrophobia much more successfully than on any other song of the period.

The Kill (aka Warsaw)

Also recorded: 12/77, Pennine Sound Studios, Oldham; 5/78, Arrow Studios, Manchester; 4/79, Strawberry Studios, Stockport

Versions available on: *An Ideal For Living, Heart And Soul, Refractured*

Yet another track that begins with Hook's simple, relentless bass, 'The Kill' (the longest number from the early Pennine Sound output) is a thoroughly rousing stab at near-Black Sabbath territory. With a demonic, descending main riff, topped with Sumner's high-pitched solo line, you get the refreshing feeling that the band really were having fun in the studio. Curtis even seems to stifle a laugh as the band collapse around him in the closing seconds.

Another reason the song sounds so successful is that it actually has a chorus, albeit a very simple one. "It's another, 'nother, 'nother, 'nother kill!" they chant in unison. It's still simple punk, but if you can rouse a crowd and forge some kind of connection with them, however sinister the implication, it won't hurt when it comes to a performance.

You're No Good For Me

'You're No Good For Me' shouldn't even have made it to demo stage. With a semi-chorus of "Na, na, na, na, na, na, na, na, no good!" and the over-used 1-2-3-4 intro, it plumbs the depths of mundanity and is really little more than identikit sub-punk. A particularly bad line comes in the fifth verse, where Curtis claims that he "can wash the dishes" and that his "soups can taste delicious." 'The Eternal' it isn't. One reviewer at the time suggested that Warsaw were "...doomed maybe to eternal support slots. Whether they will find a style of their own is questionable..." Songs like 'You're No Good For Me' would not have helped their cause.

An Ideal For Living

Recorded: 12/1977, Pennine Sound Studios, Oldham
Produced by: Warsaw
All available on: *Warsaw, Substance*

The band's first release, this EP takes the sound of the earlier, rougher punk they had been rehearsing so intensely and refines it slightly. In it a sound is created, albeit embryonically, that hints at the mournfully evocative music Warsaw and Joy Division would go on to make, but with just enough of that traditional, snarling, punk attitude left to mean the record would be largely ignored by the masses.

Warsaw

Also recorded: 5/78, Arrow Studios, Manchester; 25/7/78, Radio Manchester Session; 28/2/80, The Warehouse venue, Preston
Versions available on: *Preston 28 February 1980, Heart And Soul, Refractured*

"350125—Go!" spits Curtis at the start of the first version of the second Joy Division song to be titled 'Warsaw'. For this version, Curtis's voice is double- (and occasionally treble-) tracked, with a neatly complementary backing vocal adding cohesion to an already well-formed song. The guitar line seems to be smooth in comparison to the later Arrow Studios version, and the bass is much less dominating.

Six months later, something of the subtlety has been lost in the Arrow Studios version, perhaps a casualty of the ill feeling between band and producer which is rumored to have blighted the RCA demo sessions.

At Preston, just over two years after the initial recording, little has changed in the song, but the playing is superior (even at a gig widely regarded as poor). The number chanting is absent from the beginning again (but present at the close), and the stutter of the guitar and the pounding rhythm is very effective. Perhaps Joy Division aren't having fun, but there's a cohesion to a track like this, played so late in their career, that suggests an affection for the track not noted elsewhere.

No Love Lost
Also recorded: 05/78, Arrow Studios, Manchester; 25/7/78, Radio Manchester Session
Versions available on: *An Ideal For Living, Substance, Heart And Soul*

Like 'Warsaw' from this session, 'No Love Lost' (the title is taken from a quote from the *House Of Dolls* book which also provides the spoken passage by Curtis in the middle eight), is explicitly linked to the Nazi imagery with which the band were beginning to be awkwardly associated. In this version, the more chilling of several versions attempted, the singer tells of the "instrument which they had that morning inserted deep into her body" in a slow, heavily monotone voice. It's a disturbing moment, the effect heightened by the upbeat nature of the music.

But to focus on such ghoulishness is miss out on one of the band's most innovative early works. A long way from the thrashy punk of previous months, the first 35 seconds reveal a group experimenting on their own terms. Morris' tom drum playing is exquisite, while Sumner's mid-range guitar flirts with the continually wrong-footing bassline that begins the track. It has a cumulative effect that evolves into the main riff, but the structure remains tight underneath, especially during the spoken passage. How devastating would this song have been if Martin Hannett had got his hands on it?

Leaders Of Men
Also recorded: 05/78, Arrow Studios, Manchester, 25/7/78, Radio Manchester Session
Versions available on: *An Ideal For Living, Substance*

Live, the band was ploughing an altogether more metallic furrow, according to music journalist Mike Nicholls. "Their overall sound is grounded in the late 1970s, mainly due to the Banshee-esque metallic chord-chopping of guitarist Bernard... the Teutonic influence extends to the subject matter of most of their songs including 'Leaders Of Men', the only number I recognised from their home made *An Ideal For Living* EP."

Atonal and slow in pace, 'Leaders Of Men' has an odd charm that can still work its magic today. There's something about Curtis' delivery that sounds out of place, particularly when heard in the context of the *Heart And Soul* box set. Was he relaxed, or just not trying too hard? Could he be experimenting with a different vocal style at this very early stage of his singing career? Overall the sound is more nasal than on other Joy Division recordings, and it's one this writer wishes he had experimented with more.

Curtis' lyrics employ a number of typical Joy Division themes. There's the mention of the "crowd". Then "just a minor operation" harks back to the extract from *House Of Dolls* in 'No Love Lost'; and there's an allusion to escape, illustrated by a visit to the cinema—a place where "the future's not made".

In the first national interview for *Sounds* music paper in November 1978, Curtis told Mick Middles that the lyrics were from an old notebook and gave a glimpse into his way of working. "I have a lot of lyrics in reserve so I'll use them when the right tune comes along. The lines are usually made up of all sorts of odd bits. 'Leaders Of Men', for example—some of the lyrics are two or three years old."

The last 20 seconds of the song are noticeably lush in guitar terms, with the consistent 'traffic passing' effect (think Kraftwerk's 'Autobahn') in the higher line replaced by an introspective coda, much lower down the scale.

Failures [Of The Modern Man]
Also recorded: 05/78, Arrow Studios, Manchester; 25/7/78, Radio Manchester Session
Versions available on: *An Ideal For Living, Substance, Heart And Soul*

Usually referred as just 'Failures', this could easily be taken for a Lou Reed cover if heard booming out from a club. It's The Velvet Underground turned up a notch, more manic and exhilarating than you would expect from such an embryonic work. Yet it seems out of place—perhaps a tribute to collective influences that they had already outgrown.

A large part of the Reed similarity stems from the vocals. Curtis lengthens the first word of each line, a style that Liam Gallagher of Oasis would use (check out any Oasis greatest hits or live performance), but the trick also serves as an interesting diversion from the darker tracks from this session.

The lyrics take the form of two halves, with each line divided by the meter of the second half. In a sense this is a call-and-response lyric—as Curtis says his subject "no longer denies" or "no longer picks sides," each observation is met with the title, or a variant of it.

Knowingly or otherwise, Curtis was beginning to not only appreciate what he was singing, but also that how he sang it affected its impact. He employs repetition with slight changes in each repeat to cumulative effect, and his lyrics act in the same way as the wordless bassline. In this version, each verse sees the second half of the last line repeated. In the later Arrow studios version, each of these repeats is shorn off, which shows Curtis now knew the simpler call-and-response approach was more effective.

RCA Demo Sessions

Recorded: 5/78, Arrow Studios, Manchester
Produced by: Richard Searling, Jon Anderson, Bob Auger
All available on: *Warsaw*

Recorded as a kind of 'try out' for the RCA label, these sessions are a good example of great ideas being badly handled. The first instance of Joy Division using outside producers, these 11 tracks represent a perfect snapshot of the group at the time. There are brand new, wonderfully creative tracks ('Transmission'), nods to the now quickly receding past ('Warsaw') and several tracks that would earn a place (in re-recorded versions) on *Unknown Pleasures*.

The only problem is, given the naivety of the performers and the fact there was no clear path for the producers to follow, the results now sound half-finished or even half-hearted at times. Nevertheless, the speed at which the band was developing is clear, and the genesis of one or two Joy Division classics can be found here.

The Drawback
Also available on: *Heart And Soul*

Just 1:46 minutes in length, 'The Drawback' (occasionally referred to as 'All Of This For You') is the closest the band ever came to the sound of Buzzcocks.

A simple three-chord run-through at a frantic pace, the song is largely notable for its stop-start mechanics and the octopus-like drum fills. Yet there is something slightly overbearing about the way the track breaks down, with unnecessary pauses and, at points after 1:15, a lack of direction. Curtis' voice, with the rest of the instrumentation dropped out in the breaks towards the close, sounds weak on its own, and the speed at which the lines are delivered make the lyrics sound forced and cluttered.

Eight of the lines in this short song begin with either "I've seen..." or "I've had..."—a witnessing technique Curtis would develop as the months drew on. Here Curtis views injustices and moral problems, and hints that his viewpoint comes from a time in the future, or that he himself is looking back through time ("I've seen what's left of poor technology and work"). It's a lofty standpoint, but it works in the context of the music.

Leaders Of Men

Also recorded: 12/1977, Pennine Sound Studios, Oldham; 25/7/78, Radio Manchester Session
Versions available on: *An Ideal For Living, Heart And Soul*

Oddly, this later version cannot touch the one recorded six months earlier for *An Ideal For Living*. Admittedly it's only a demo, but there seems to have been something of a step backwards. Curtis sings in the more familiar concerned tone of the more upbeat side of *Unknown Pleasures*, and the excellent guitar line is too dominating to impress as fully as it did before. Morris' drums also appear to be badly recorded, with hiss from the hi-hat cymbals replacing the wonderful thud of the bass drum of the earlier incarnation.

But despite such disappointments, there are still redeeming features. Curtis turns in a confident performance, at ease with the structure of the song and the meter of the lyric, and Sumner's change in guitar at 2:04 brings to mind one or two of the tricks of The Smiths' Johnny Marr—except they're being done five years earlier.

[They] Walked In Line
Also recorded: 04/79, Strawberry Studios, Stockport
Versions available on: *Still, Heart And Soul*

Close kin to 'Shadowplay', 'Walked In Line' has that trademark Joy Division 16-beat rhythm, and with Sumner's guitar
also following the familiar slash/change chord/slash pattern,
it's perhaps not surprising that this song went no further.

But there are positive sides too. Curtis seems to be really
finding his voice—joyously it's the laconic, withdrawn style
used to such good effect on 'Inside The Line'—and he
sounds comfortable with the army of replicas behind him in
the main line of the chorus (simply the title repeated). The
version here has an extended second verse, but not the
military-style drum rolls that would pepper the Strawberry
Studios version.

Lyrically, it's another gloomy, apparently military, setting. Regardless of the identity of the men who "killed to
pass the time", the scene painted is bleak, one of resigna-
tion and numbed obedience. From the very title, the char-
acters within the story are obeying orders. But Curtis as
storyteller never glorifies them; he merely seems dumb-
founded at their lives. Maybe the spirit of punk, one of
individuality and following your own path—ideals to
which Curtis clung, made regimented procedures more
baffling. These are not specifically Nazi officers Curtis is
studying—nowhere does he mention race, style of uniform
or even something as obvious as a swastika—so 'Walked In
Line' seems to be a genuine fascination.

Failures

Also recorded: 12/1977, Pennine Sound Studios, Oldham;
25/7/78, Radio Manchester Session
Versions available on: *An Ideal For Living, Substance, Heart And Soul*

There is little difference in actual playing between this version and the one recorded at Pennine Sound, but here there is less reliance from Curtis on drawing out his words. The pace remains scintillatingly fast, with the vocals starting before the instruments, acting as a count-in. The sound is overly trebly, with an indulgent guitar solo at the close and the now omnipresent hi-hat sizzling across the two-and-a-half minutes.

The vocals have a clarity, however, and betray a hitherto hidden manic edge to the lyrics, with their tales of Caesar and false messiahs. But the song sounds under-rehearsed, with a fuzzy chaos towards the closing seconds, wherein the band seem to just guess where they should end, independently of one another. Perhaps the attempt is more indicative of the band live at the time, rushed and nerve-ridden, rather than studied and measured.

Novelty

Also recorded: 07/79, Central Studios, Manchester (unreleased), 13/7/79, The Factory Club, Manchester; 07/79, Strawberry Studios, Stockport
Versions available on: 'Transmission' single, *Substance, Permanent, Heart And Soul*

Sounding not unlike The Beatles' 'I Want You (She's So Heavy)' at its opening, the song quickly turns into a vicious diatribe which uses the descending chord structure which the band were beginning to find second nature. At points Curtis is so crystal clear in the mix that it seems the other members have been turned down (just listen to the line "You're the only one now…"), but on the whole this is the sound of an increasingly confident band. It's still a work in progress, however. The lyrics would take on at least another two recorded forms.

The altogether rougher version recorded at The Factory Club, introduced as "a very old song, some of you might remember it," is practically a different number altogether, so forcefully is it played. Sumner's guitar is ridiculously high in the mix, but more searing are Curtis' vocals. Rendered more intense by the sound quality, they nevertheless almost scorch the eardrums in their high-pitched scream.

Lyrically, 'Novelty' is unique in that it undergoes three changes over its lifespan. By the time of the live version here, Curtis has shown finesse in his tweaking of lines like "When the novelty has gone" to the more typically Joy Division "when the novelty fades away." The first verse is changed too, with the identikit punk of "you've got to work so hard for everything you've got" changed to the far subtler "All the dreams you ever had are tied up deep inside." It's a strong sign that the band did not rest on tried and tested formulas if they were not completely satisfied.

No Love Lost
Also recorded: 12/77, Pennine Sound Studios, Oldham;
25/7/78, Radio Manchester Session

Versions available on: *An Ideal For Living, Substance, Heart And Soul*

At just nine seconds short of five minutes, this version is a real secret weapon in the band's canon. The most obvious use of producer Jon Anderson's beloved keyboards can be heard across the disco-lite intro, only offset by the jarring guitar that scrapes away behind. The bass is now less dominant, so much so as to be almost inaudible, but the beat-skipping, with the emphasis on fourth beat of every bar, makes for an almost prog-rock experience. This time around we don't even hear a peep from Curtis until around 3:30.

The break at 1:30 is pure Velvet Underground, a simple, brazen power chord strum, but it's neither over the top nor superfluous. In the passage that follows before the vocal, some discordant scratches, like a flock of seagulls, from Bernard, help to build the tension. The same can't be said of the drum solo at 4:09, however.

The reading from Karol Cetinsky's *House Of Dolls* is left out in this version. It's replaced by another verse, which talks about slightly less ghoulish (but equally sinister) "two-way mirrors" and hidden "transmitters".

Which leads us neatly on to...

Transmission
Also recorded: 31/1/79, Maida Vale Studios, London; 4/3/79, Eden Studios London; 7/79, Central Sound Studios, Manchester; 8/79, Strawberry Studios, Stockport; 13/7/79, The Factory Club, Manchester; 15/9/79, *Something Else* Studios; 18/12/79, Les Bains Douches, Paris; 11/1/80, The

Paradiso Club, Amsterdam; 28/2/80, The Warehouse venue, Preston; 2/5/80, Birmingham University
Versions available on: Single release, 'Atmosphere' single release, 'Love Will Tear Us Apart' single release, *Peel Sessions*, *The Complete BBC Recordings*, *Still*, *Substance*, *Permanent*, *Preston 28 February 1980*, *Heart And Soul*, *Les Bains Douches 18 December 1979*, *Before And After*, *Refractured*

'Transmission' remains a vital turning point for the band's psyche. As Peter Hook recounted to Mick Middles in 1996, "we played a gig at The Mayflower, and when we were sound-checking we launched into 'Transmission' and all the other musicians, sound crew, everyone, just stopped and looked at us. I looked at Barney and Barney looked at me saying, 'Fuuuuuckin' hell, we've really got something here.' That's when it really hit me. I never thought we were special before that."

It would be great to say that 'Transmission'—one of Joy Division's pivotal singles and a song that remains ingrained in the mind's eye because of Curtis' fabulously morbid dance—was genius from conception. But the version recorded at Arrow shows that it took work. Peter Hook starts this version as he did on the final one, only he has yet to hold that important note at the start of each bar, rendering the bassline somewhat anaemic by comparison. When Morris comes in, his drums sound too cymbal-heavy, and worst of all is the synthizer, which does its best to make proceedings sound spaced-out and trippy but instead just means that this version has aged, badly.

There is none of the frantic tension of the final release; even the guitar line that laced the eventual masterwork seems sloppy and stoned here. If it was Anderson's intention to make a record that mirrored and marvelled at the radio age, then his attempts at mimicking the sounds of interference and static by using a synthesizer and the parts of a guitar string above the nut (most annoyingly just after Curtis sings the word "radio") are sadly misplaced.

The performers are not without blame either. For much of the time Curtis sounds as if he's firing on half his cylinders. The pace really needs to be injected with the power that the final version has (thanks to Morris' exciting drum track, which is much better heard on the version from Paris), and Sumner has yet to create the screeching, wailing, guitar response that would come in just after Curtis has screamed "Dance!".

That said, 'Transmission' as a statement of intent is a fine signpost. As a canny summation of American influences, it delivers a sound and a space more in keeping with the New York noiseniks that Curtis et al held so dear. As Adam Sweeting of the *NME* noted in a review of the band at a Factory Moonlight concert in August 1979: "Gothic yells of 'I put my trust in you!' lined up alongside the thudding bass riff of 'Transmission'. An encore of the Velvets' 'Sister Ray' made explicit Joy Division's earlier hints at a very American spaciousness."

The American comparison was continued much later, in the *NME* of 19 April 1980, when Neil Norman noted that "they are the only group who deserve to be framed within the same context as The Velvet Underground and The Doors." Max Bell, reviewing the band's debut earlier in the same paper in July 1979, would later breathlessly conclude that "[*Unknown Pleasures*'] only equivalent [is] probably made in

Los Angeles, twelve years earlier: The Doors' *LA Woman*…
[It is] the most pertinent comparison I can make…"

Lyrically, 'Transmission' is interesting for its snapshot approach. The opening words of "Radio—live transmission" could come straight from the red light on the door of a studio and is wonderfully evocative. It acts as a buzzing intro, an almost visual place in time returned to before each verse. But most memorable of all is the chant of "Dance, dance, dance" that echoes across the frenzy of Morris' drum collapse behind. This line seems to have been frozen in time, somehow fused with the Curtis persona onstage, himself dancing in the mind's eye of every Joy Division fan.

Live, too, the band were affecting writers. The *NME*, describing a hometown gig in September 1978, wrote: "In months they have matured considerably. They have learnt to sculpt, not merely to emit. They are now not instinctively fast and frenzied… [They have] been lifted out of a surrounding morass of clumsiness and unsureness and elaborated on, sharpened up… from a punk group with minimal awareness and ability to a music group with eloquence and direction."

Ice Age
Also recorded: 4/3/79, Eden Studios, London; 11/79, Cargo Studios, Rochdale
Versions available on: *Still, Heart And Soul*

In all the recorded output from this period, the spectre of The Stooges hangs heaviest of all over 'Ice Age'. With its primal use of the tom drums throughout, and a unique (for Joy Division) choral hook (again, just the title of the song repeated), it's something of a Warsaw/Joy Division oddity. Audaciously simple, the song uses its own momentum as a catalyst for soloing and experimentation, and there is a comfort evident among the players that would seem to contradict the angst of punk or the social turmoil individual members were experiencing.

The first 15 seconds alone are exciting enough, with a humming bass drum and a Bond theme guitar chiming away. Curtis spits his lyric about atrocities buried in the sand (which would later be scratched in the run-out groove to the 'Transmission' single) well beneath the other parts, and is almost whispering at points. Then at 0:36 he comes further forward with his enigmatic chant of "Nothing will hold, nothing will fit."

The lyrics point towards the future of Joy Division— sparse and minimal, and are a hint that Curtis need not cram so many words into a verse to achieve a poetic effect. Indeed, the second verse has just 12 words. Discomfort and unrest hang heavy, and the theme of being a misfit or outcast seeps through. The song seems to be pointed at an individual or partner, with the narrator holding hands with them in the first verse, but any warmth is lost by the close, with "Into the cold, no smile on your lips"—an allusion to the title.

Interzone
Also recorded: 04/79, Strawberry Studios, Stockport;
13/7/79, The Factory Club, Manchester; 9/79, *Rock On*,
Radio 1 studios; 11/1/80, The Paradiso Club, Amsterdam;
28/2/80, The Warehouse venue, Preston
Versions available on: *Unknown Pleasures, Preston 28 February
1980, Heart And Soul, Refractured*

Sounding somewhat crude in this format, the song that will sit second-from-last on *Unknown Pleasures* here features just a single set of lyrics (Peter Hook would go on to sing a 'response' to each line when it was played live) and little of the mysticism that made the definitive version. Shorn of Martin Hannett's magic touch (remember that the production here was being handled by the soul-oriented trio of Anderson, Searling and Auger), the haunting, wailing background noise is revealed to be merely Curtis, not some ghostly banshee from the moors, while Sumner's guitar is enormously over the top, yet still clinical and cold in its production.

The mystical, wordless, chanting that sounds so effective on the *Unknown Pleasures* version is still present, but stripped of effects and at points aping the guitar melody, it sounds almost comic here. At the final few bars the immediacy of the end chord is lost, the band choosing instead to let the track come to a natural close rather than the sharp, punctuated, burst that would later emerge so successfully.

Other than that, the song changes little instrumentally from studio version to live version, but if the recordings are listened to in chronological order, the good work a producer can do becomes very apparent.

Warsaw
Also recorded: 7/77, Pennine Sound Studios, Oldham; 12/77, Pennine Sound Studios, Oldham; 4/79, Strawberry Studios, Stockport; 28/2/80, The Warehouse venue, Preston
Versions available on: *An Ideal For Living, Preston 28 February 1980, Refractured*

Stripped of the prisoner number at the beginning, 'Warsaw' makes for interesting listening as a benchmark of just how far the band had come in six months. Of all Warsaw's early work, it's most easy to imagine this track (in polished, Hannett-produced, form at least) making it on to *Unknown Pleasures*.

The chord progression is bracing, especially in the perfunctory chorus, behind the cries of "3-1-G", and the balance of instruments competing for attention is well levelled out. The intro is the best example of this, with a solo, scratchy guitar for five seconds building to the riff, before a bulb of bass is brought out a smidgen under Morris' rasping hi-hat work.

The drop to minor chords for the chorus also heightens the effect of this relatively simple progression beautifully. Warsaw are becoming songwriters before our very ears, and it's great to hear.

Lyrically the heat is turned up too. Curtis' skill at placing the reader in the situation of the narrator, yet retaining a cold distance, is already in effect. "I can still hear the footsteps, I can see only walls, I slid into your man-traps, with no hearing at all" may be lacking in subtlety, but in just two lines he manages to elicit pity, confusion, guilt and trepidation. No mean feat.

Shadowplay
Also recorded: 20/8/79, Granada TV Studios, Manchester; 4/79, Strawberry Studios, Stockport; 9/79, *Rock On*, Radio 1 studios; 18/12/79, Les Bains Douches, Paris; 11/1/80, The Paradiso Club, Amsterdam; 28/2/80, The Warehouse venue, Preston; 2/5/80, Birmingham University

Versions available on: *Preston 28 February 1980, Heart And Soul, Les Bains Douches 18 December 1979, Unknown Pleasures, Refractured*

When listening to this version of 'Shadowplay' back-to-back with the one on *Unknown Pleasures*, what Martin Hannett did at Strawberry becomes slightly clearer. With little difference in what was sung and done between each version (save for a 15-second time difference), the success of the finished version clearly lies in the production.

In this version the levels are recorded wrongly. Curtis doesn't yet sound completely comfortable in his voice (in Paris, this problem solved, he would confidently yell "turn the vocals up, please!"), while the sheet-glass guitar line from Sumner is buried so far down in the sludge of bass that it's practically inaudible.

Also, there are none of the 'explosive' noises that would work so well later, and the double-tracking of the vocals on the "I did everything..." lines has yet to be employed.

There is a climactic play around the cymbals from Morris at the beginning, and the crescendo builds three or four times before the main rhythm commences, although this is some-what anti-climactic when it does arrive.

It must also be said that Curtis is rarely in tune with the band here, although at the beginning of many lines there is a sharp edge to his vocal that is suitably menacing in the context of the lyrics. At the "I did everything" section he even comes across as sarcastic, although any intimidation is lost with a completely superfluous echo effect by the time he reaches the line "waiting for you."

A Factory Sample

Recorded: 11/10/78, Cargo Studios, Rochdale
Produced by: Martin Hannett
All available on: *A Factory Sample*

Martin Hannett's first production efforts for Joy Division resulted in two of the Joy Division tracks most loved by fans. The idea may have been as much about creating an identity for the new Factory label as promoting the four acts on the double-pack EP, but 'Glass'—and 'Digital' in particular—are the best signposts one could hope for that something special was just around the corner. This is where Joy Division really began, their confidence growing rapidly and their sound becoming more their own.

Digital

Also recorded: 4/3/79, Eden Studios, London; 11/1/80, The Paradiso Club, Amsterdam; 18/1/80, De Effenaar, Eindhoven; 2/5/80, Birmingham University
Versions available on: *Still, Heart And Soul, Les Bains Douches 18 December 1979, Refractured*

'Digital' is the first real sign, however embryonic, of Joy Division beginning to appreciate space in a recording. This was largely due to Hannett, who would reveal to Jon Savage: "There was lots of space in their sound initially... There used to be a lot of room in the music, and they were a gift to a producer, 'cos they didn't have a clue."

The simplest of drum beats (a bass drum, a snare and an alternate thwack of the hi-hat) coupled with a repetitive bassline that doesn't need to do anything else, were all matched with a vocal that could rouse even the sleepiest of listeners. The repetition of the line "Day in, day out" quickens the pulse, especially as Curtis gets more and more fearful in his everyday terror. Once again the overall effect is akin to claustrophobia.

On the Eindhoven performance, Hook teases the crowd with a plodding, two-note extended intro (although this has often been explained as the bassist freezing to the spot in reaction to a situation in the crowd). Most significant on this version is the scorch of Curtis in the chorus, an already drained PA and recording device pushed to its limits by a human, not by any of the machines present.

The lyrics form a devastating complement to the fraught tempo and climactic music. The "day in day out" refrain could be heard as the cry of "the in, the out"—a dark slang phrase in A Clockwork Orange's droog-speak meaning sexual intercourse. There is also a genuine human passion free of the cold suffocation evident in earlier lines ("I feel it closing in") in what Curtis sings at the close: he admits to needing something or someone for a change, rather than craving solitude. "Don't ever fade away, I need you here today," he yells at increasing volumes, sounding desperately anxious.

If you wanted to make a record that would be your debut for a label that would be remembered largely for your existence, you couldn't really ask for any more than 'Digital'.

Glass
Also recorded: 4/3/79, Eden Studios, London
Versions available on: Still, Substance, Heart And Soul, Peel Sessions, The Complete BBC Recordings

'Glass' differs from 'Digital' in the way so much seems to be going on, in the first minute alone. When Curtis wails for the first time after 50 seconds, we've already heard car-alarm guitars, minimalist abstract lyrics, the sound of a march going by, discordant slams, a furious 16-beat, a doodling squiggle of a bassline, handclaps, squeaks and what can only be breaking glass. Somehow this scatter approach works, as any initial sense of being overwhelmed soon gives way to a familiarity and desire to hear where the band and producer will take it next.

Curtis is on fine form, part-singing, part-instructing his way through a skeletal lyric. A word-heavy lyric would not sit well with the sparseness of the instrumentation, so a simple line like "Hearts fail—young hearts fail" is far more effective. Curtis is clearly listening to the music the band is making before setting down a lyric. Even "overheat, overtired" says enough in this context to make a point.

A Factory Sample was well received, with one reviewer singling out Joy Division: "[They] wind their claustrophobic, abrasive yet precise anger even tighter, a quality only hinted at on their previous EP. Both 'Digital' and 'Glass' are strong, massive, and... make you want to hear more."

Peel Session 1
Recorded: 31/1/79, Maida Vale Studios, London
Produced by: Bob Sargent, engineered by Nick Gomm
All available on: *Peel Sessions, The Complete BBC Recordings*

The opportunity for a band to record a session for the late British Radio 1 DJ John Peel meant many things. It was an acknowledgement of your work from a highly respected source—the man was already well on his way to becoming a national musical instititution—and the chance to join the list of 'cool' acts who had already received that accolade.

It also provided vital public exposure and perhaps just as important, free studio time and a chance to road-test new songs that the acts had not yet recorded.

All these aspects are evident on the first of two sessions that Joy Division recorded for the station. One only needs to listen to the 'nearly there' version of 'Transmission' to appreciate the rate at which they were developing, and the ideas which they were now beginning to fine-tune.

Exercise One

Also recorded: 4/79, Strawberry Studios, Stockport
Versions available on: *Still, Heart And Soul, Before And After*

Something about the balance of the instruments on the band's first Peel session makes for a compelling listen. From the 20-second screech of feedback at its opening, 'Exercise One' reeks of menace. Sumner's guitar dominates, with a chiming and climactic riff that pervades right the way through to the brutal cut out at 2:32. Hook's bass is as low as ever, while Morris plays a comparatively simple beat, merely underpinning the sound.

Curtis' lyrical prowess and morbid fascination really come to the fore here. The lines "Turn away from it all—it's all getting too much/When you're looking at life, deciphering scars" do more than hint at an inability to cope, and even suggest a slight sense of self-loathing. Moreover, this succinct song has just two short verses—the up-front abruptness of punk is giving way to a painful understanding that what is left out of a lyric is just as important as what goes into it.

Insight

Also recorded: 4/3/79, Eden Studios, London; 4/79, Strawberry Studios, Stockport; 13/7/79, The Factory Club, Manchester; 18/12/79, Les Bains Douches, Paris

Versions available on: *Unknown Pleasures, Heart And Soul, Les Bains Douches 18 December 1979, Before And After, Refractured*

In his sleevenotes to the 2000 *Complete BBC Recordings* CD, Dave Simpson of *The Guardian* calls these Peel sessions "an image of remarkable perfection." Something about the balance between the wondrous underwater guitar sounds and the shrill synthesizer that constantly shifts from left to right makes this far superior to the version on *Unknown Pleasures*. Certainly there are wrinkles to be smoothed out (why the drums, and the cymbals especially, are so trebly and high in the mix is anyone's guess), but the structure is practically there, and there is a jaunty freshness that's irresistible.

Curtis seems content in the lyrics, but deviates slightly in delivery. His cries of "I'm not afraid any more", after 2:55 especially, are carefree and practically shouted.

As Chris Bohn wrote in his review of the group playing at the University of London Union: "In other hands their songs would collapse disastrously. But Curtis's controlled balladeering makes lines like 'I remember/when we were young' sound like one of the saddest statements in pop, which is, after all, the province of the young, and that sung to the sweetest, most melancholic tune too."

She's Lost Control

Also recorded: 4/79, Strawberry Studios, Stockport;
13/7/79, The Factory Club, Manchester; 19/7/79, Granada
TV Studios, Manchester; 15/9/79, BBC 2 Studios,
Manchester; 11/1/80, The Paradiso Club, Amsterdam;
28/2/80, The Warehouse venue, Preston; 29/2/80, The
Lyceum, London; 3/80, Strawberry Studios, Stockport
Versions available on: Single release, *Unknown Pleasures,
Substance, Permanent, Preston 28 February 1980, Heart And Soul,
Before And After, Refractured*

The most immediate difference on this version is the unsub-
merged trigger that Morris uses at the start of each bar,
sounding like a key being smacked against the inside of a full
bath rather than the equivalent higher-pitched, clinking
smack that surfaces on *Unknown Pleasures*. Elsewhere, Morris
sounds less rigid in his playing, freed up by the continual
fast drum fills.

Also, towards the turn of the fourth minute, Hook and
Sumner seem to act independently of one another. With an
already meandering pace, not helped by the illusion of a rigid
beat, this version pales in comparison to the one that would
appear on *Unknown Pleasures*. No one band member seems
completely comfortable, and much as a feeling of discomfort
is what one might expect when listening to Joy Division, the
Martin Hannett version wins every time.

Transmission

Also recorded: 5/78, Arrow Studios, Manchester; 4/3/79,
Eden Studios, London; 7/79, Central Studios, Manchester;

8/79, Strawberry Studios, Stockport; 13/7/79, The Factory
Club, Manchester; 15/9/79, BBC 2 Studios, Manchester;
18/12/79, Les Bains Douches, Paris; 11/1/80, The Paradiso
Club, Amsterdam; 28/2/80, The Warehouse venue, Preston;
2/5/80, Birmingham University
Versions available on: Single release, 'Atmosphere' single
release, 'Love Will Tear Us Apart' single release, *Substance,
Permanent, Preston 28 February 1980, Heart And Soul, Les Bains
Douches 18 December 1979, Before And After, Refractured*

On 'Insight', Stephen Morris' drums were mixed so high that
they were overpowering, but here they're nearly excluded
from the other instruments. It makes for an interesting
version of this song. Peter Hook still appears to be trying to
find the perfect number of bass 'syllables', while Morris' part
is virtually forming before our ears. With each roll of the
drum, a little more of the finished article is pieced together.
Just listening to the tom drum at the close is enough to
make you feel you're in the studio with the band, so cleanly
is it recorded.

At 0:53 Sumner seems to try a different guitar part by
picking at his strings, but this is only half effective. Later the
guitar seems to get in the way, when Curtis reaches his "beat
of the drum" lyric, but later still, at 3:03, the singer triumphs
with the consistently breathtaking cry of "Daaaaance!". At
the close, Morris' drums, slowly decreasing in speed, fade to
one final pop on the tom.

While no longer a work in progress, 'Transmission' at the
Beeb still needs one or two aspects tightening up, but remains
a fascinating document in this form.

The Genetic Recordings

Recorded: 4/3/79, Eden Studios, London
Produced by: Martin Rushent
All available on: All except 'Digital' appear on *Heart And Soul*

The Genetic recordings are a weird pit-stop in the Joy Division story. Having already worked successfully with Martin Hannett, the choice of Martin Rushent as producer seems an odd one. Perhaps the band were impressed by the commercial success he had achieved as producer of Buzzcocks and were thinking about a similar breakthrough. Yet none of the tracks recorded here have the impact of their Hannett equivalents, and the only real change one can sense is the growing ability of Ian Curtis behind the microphone—his voice practically strengthens with each line. But mistakes abound, from both producer and band, and as if to illustrate that this is not one of the group's best sessions, the version of 'Digital' recorded here has never been officially released.

Insight

Also recorded: 31/1/79, BBC Maida Vale Studios, London; 4/79, Strawberry Studios, Stockport; 13/7/79, The Factory Club, Manchester; 18/12/79, Les Bains Douches, Paris
Versions available on: *Unknown Pleasures, Peel Sessions, The Complete BBC Recordings, Heart And Soul, Les Bains Douches 18 December 1979, Before And After, Refractured*

The first thing one notices about the production in the Eden sessions is that the drums just don't sound as good as those on their album and single counterparts. Structurally, 'Insight' is identical to the version on *Unknown Pleasures*: all the actual components are in place, but the space between them has yet to be arrived at. For instance, an effect has been placed on the bass drum, but very little, if any, on the snare. Doing the reverse would become part of the band's success story.

Also, the crazed stabs of keyboards in the two bridges are revealed to be little more than percussive bursts that follow the bass line, whereas on the later, Hannett-produced effort, the chaos evident was clearly a studio construction rather than haphazard playing.

That this version is more ponderous than the album version is largely due to the predominance of Sumner's simple guitar picking, and the comparatively low mix of that threatening bass. There's also a relative confusion in the space between the instruments. The synthesizers, so striking and unexpected on the album, seem clumsy and lacking in subtlety here. The menace from Hook's bass, given room to breathe in the loop after the synth 'wig out' on the album, is not yet in place, and a sense of being 'almost there' runs throughout this recording.

Glass

Also recorded: 11/10/78, Cargo Studios, Rochdale

Versions available on: *A Factory Sample, Still, Substance, Heart And Soul*

There is a certain charm to the Genetic recording of 'Glass' that comes from the murkiness of the production, with the simplicity of the guitar line magnified by the lack of Hannett's sheen and effects. The bass, however, sounds terribly plodding, and is extremely high in the mix for a part so clearly below par. It would almost have been better to leave it off entirely.

Shorn of the effects that made the version on *A Factory Sample* so arresting, the song stands revealed as somewhat ungainly. The instruments are forced to over-compensate for the absence of studio trickery, the cymbals attempting to replicate the marching and clapping sounds from the Hannett version and the guitar struggling to fill the gaps left by the synths and phasing. Once again, the band seem not quite to know when the song should end, and the crash of cymbals on the very last beat comes as a welcome relief after a tense ride. In this form, 'Glass' is something like a triumph of adversity over chaos.

Digital

Also recorded: 11/10/78, Cargo Studios, Rochdale; 11/1/80, The Paradiso Club, Amsterdam; 18/1/80, De Effenaar, Eindhoven; 2/5/80, Birmingham University
Versions available on: *A Factory Sample, Still, Substance, Heart And Soul, Les Bains Douches 18 December 1979, Refractured*

This version has yet to find its way on to an official release—an indication, perhaps, of how poorly it is regarded by those in the band's camp. It appears on numerous bootlegs.

Ice Age

Also recorded: 5/78, Arrow Studios, Manchester; 10/79, Cargo Studios, Rochdale
Versions available on: *Still, Warsaw, Heart And Soul*

The first thing one notices is the absence of backing vocals compared to the Warsaw run-through. The urgency and pace of the previous rhythm have gone as well, and if anything Curtis sounds separated from his bandmates. Perhaps this is evidence that his voice has outgrown the older songs, and it is here that such anomalies are most apparent.

Clearly Curtis was now streets ahead of the novice punk once uncomfortable about—and in—his own voice. In fact, the vocals are really the only memorable aspect of this version. The band abandoned the attempt, and the buried guitar lines, muddled drums and ridiculously prominent bass show they were right to do so.

Transmission

Also recorded: 5/78, Arrow Studios, Manchester; 7/79, Central Sound Studios, Manchester; 8/79, Strawberry Studios, Stockport; 13/7/79, The Factory Club, Manchester; 15/9/79, BBC 2 Studios, Manchester; 11/1/80, The Paradiso Club, Amsterdam; 18/12/79, Les Bains Douches, Paris; 28/2/80, The Warehouse venue, Preston; 2/5/80, Birmingham University

Versions available on: Single release, 'Atmosphere' single release, 'Love Will Tear Us Apart' single release, *Substance, Permanent, Preston 28 February 1980, Heart And Soul, Les Bains Douches 18 December 1979, Before And After, Refractured*

It's no surprise that the drums on the Rushent-produced 'Transmission' single are markedly different to those on the final version, as most of the tracks from this session throw up discrepancies in that area. Here they are more relaxed than the definitive version, starting with a clattering half-fill that would have been better omitted. There is little of the tension in Curtis' voice that would so dominate later recordings, but this can be put down partly to the remarkably fast rate at which he was developing as a vocalist.

track by track: unknown pleasures and beyond

"I did everything"

> "Joy Division made us pick up our instruments"
>
> *Shaun Ryder, poet, Manchester, 2004*

Unknown Pleasures

Recorded: 4/79, Strawberry Studios, Stockport
Produced by: Martin Hannett, engineered by Chris Nagle
All available on: Album release, *Heart And Soul*

Their debut album came at precisely the right time for Joy Division. Having decided on a producer, label and a good selection of songs for possible inclusion, the group were poised to create an identity for themselves. On record at least, the brash, adolescent, punks were replaced by moody, often introspective, young men. Songs that had often been played live now received the Martin Hannett production treatment—tracks once familiar now ventured into new territories via synthizers, drum treatments and fabulous, wide open, spaces.

As a first album, *Unknown Pleasures* takes some beating. The work seems free of the mistakes of youth, yet still retains a freshness that can only come from a debut album. A sense of scope and possibility pervades each track, however downbeat: these were musicians still finding their feet but pursuing lofty ambitions. The observation that their heads moved faster than their feet is nowhere better illustrated than on *Unknown Pleasures*.

A note on tracks and tracklisting differences

Of the 16 tracks recorded at the *Unknown Pleasures* sessions, only 10 made the final album. Of the others, 'Autosuggestion' and 'From Safety To Where...?' ended up on the *Earcom 2: Contradiction* compilation, released by the Edinburgh-based independent Fast Product in October 1979. The remaining four wound up on the *Heart And Soul* box set of 1997.

It's interesting to note that when Peter Saville was given the tracklisting to prepare the album's artwork, the first side was sequenced differently. 'Disorder' opened the album but 'Insight' was placed second, followed by 'Day Of The Lords' and then 'Candidate'. 'New Dawn Fades' remained in its place. It must have been felt that the comparative 'jam' feel of 'Insight' would sit better in fourth place, rather than directly after the opening blast of 'Disorder'.

A note on the studios used

Peter Wadsworth, archivist of 10cc and their Strawberry Studios, notes that "Strawberry, in the 1970s and early 1980s, was the major studio of the north. There were other studios, but this was the main 'professional' studio in that region.

The fact that Joy Division also recorded in Rochdale proves this, but there is a quote where Bernard admits that he didn't really like Pennine, and that Strawberry was 'friendlier'.

"Strawberry was very up-market on the inside because of the amount of money that 10cc had spent equipping the studio. They had owned and progressed it (with a friend, Peter Tattersall) from 1968 onwards and they were well known for pumping their money into the studio rather than any extravagant rock 'n' roll lifestyle. As a result, their studio was well equipped and the control room had been redeveloped by the famous studio designers, Westlake Audio. The sound of the studio has been described as rich, plush and professional, and the most famous example of the sound (and 10cc) is the 1975 number one hit, 'I'm Not In Love'.

"By the time Joy Division were recording there, 10cc had left their Stockport studio behind and built a new Strawberry (called Strawberry South) in Dorking, Surrey. Their next number one hit ('Dreadlock Holiday') was recorded at this new venue, yet the sound is very similar to the Stockport equivalent, mainly because they again used Westlake for the design and replicated a lot of the equipment used in Strawberry North (as the Stockport studio became known). Peter Tattersall has since spoken of Martin Hannett becoming almost the Strawberry North house engineer."

Disorder
Also recorded: 13/7/79, The Factory Club, Manchester; 18/12/79, Les Bains Douches, Paris; 28/2/80, The Warehouse venue, Preston; 11/1/80, The Paradiso Club, Amsterdam; 2/5/80, Birmingham University

Versions available on: *Still, Preston 28 February 1980, Les Bains Douches 18 December 1979, Heart And Soul, Refractured*

On the Paris version of 'Disorder', the listener gets a true sense of the power of Joy Division live. Faster than the album equivalent, more distorted of bass, shriller in its guitar and seethingly furious when it comes to rhythm, the track virtually leaps from the speakers. Most interestingly, Curtis' vocal comes across as one of isolation from the rest of the group— a distant and relaxed tone at odds with the chaos around him. Not until the last three lines does he truly let go.

The Hulme (Factory Club) version takes all the above and hammers them home further still. Wilfully discordant, vocally slightly out of time and underpinned by a scathing synth that's reminiscent of a log being sawn in half, it's a ferocious rendition at odds with Curtis' matter of fact introduction. At the close, on the final repeat of the word "feeling", he even chances a soulful, solo stab at the lyric after the drums have crashed to a finish—a colorful flourish in a fraught performance.

The more familiar version on *Unknown Pleasures* is the perfect way to begin the album. Hannett's delay effects on the snare drum are pushed to the forefront by making the kit the only instrument we hear for the first six seconds, and then, just after the bass enters at that point, we hear the first burst of synthesizer. Throughout, Hook's bass, which doesn't deviate from its contrasting high/low pitch fluctuation until 2:57, competes for attention with *that* beat.

'Disorder' is the most consistently danceable track Joy Division ever laid down, and the main reason for that is Stephen Morris. The comparatively simple motif that

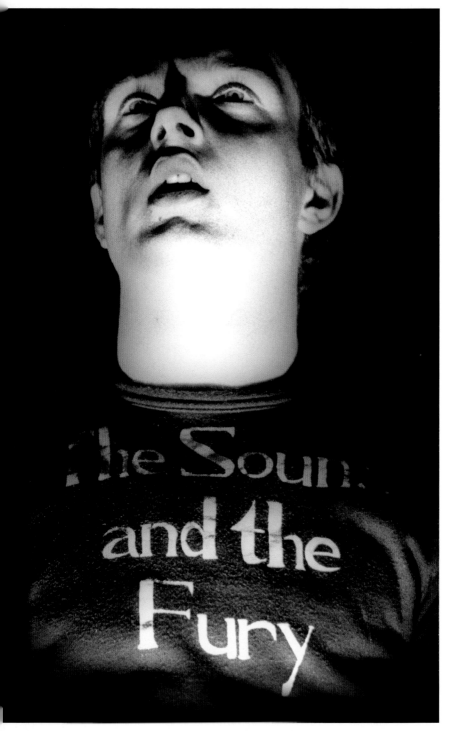

An atmospheric shot of Joy Division's main man Ian Curtis taken by photographer Lex Van Rossen.

Joy Divison (left to right) Ian Curtis, Bernard Sumner, Stephen Morris, and Peter Hook.

Once described as the "gaunt, isolated focal point" of Joy Division, Ian Curtis at the microphone.

Factory Records founder and inspiration Tony Wilson (center) with Peter Saville and Alan Erasmus.

Unknown Pleasures *producer Martin Hannett at the mixing console.*

Joy Divison's
anchorman, bass
player Peter Hook.
13 July, 1979.

(left to right) Stephen Morris, Ian Curtis, and Bernard Sumner discussing tactics in the studio.

*Ian Curtis on stage,
not long after the
June 1979 release of
Unknown Pleasures
to huge critical
acclaim. 13 July,
1979.*

*Guitar man Bernard
Sumner, as above an
in-concert shot by
Kevin Cummins.
13 July, 1979.*

Ian Curtis out in front, with Bernard Sumner in the foreground, at a live date in March 1979.

introduces the song turns into a hybrid with an ornate hi-hat shuffle, accentuated with a lift of the left foot for the last two beats of each bar—something of a drumming feat that goes against the natural desire to keep a constant rhythm. This slight pause, or softer sound, provides a platform from which to take in the rest of the instruments.

If the bass and drums are what we pick up on initially, Sumner's memorable guitar at the 57-second mark is surely what we take away. A sweeping, luxurious, riff contrasting with the heightened tension of the rhythm, it is practically a solo, were it not that the other musicians don't take a back-seat to allow the guitarist room. By the close, when Morris continually rolls across his kit, Sumner is well into a Fall-style riff, lower in the mix, scratchy but part of the foundations. As tinny as ever, it lies behind the great grey wash of synth, which only fades out after everything else has gone silent.

It's odd, but one can almost hear strains of disco in 'Disorder', and the keyboards—floating eerily above the mix, subtle at first but all-pervading for the final minute—seem to represent a manifesto of sorts. Yes, they have made a song that you will want to move to, but you will also want to think about it long after the dancing has stopped.

The lyrics help, of course. By now, Curtis had truly come into his own as a writer. On 'Disorder' he takes the listener through a dizzying volley of imagery, but still manages to intersperse this abstraction with a coherent, despairing narrative. "New sensations barely interest me for another day," he sings, and seeks a guide to help. In the second verse, things take a turn for the worse—"It's getting out of hand… Lights are flashing, cars are crashing, getting frequent now,

I've got the spirit, lose the feeling..." Surely this is a veiled reference to epilepsy? At the end the narrator, sensing the futility of man's existence, pleads that he has the spirit, but either wants to lose the feeling, or keeps losing it. Either way, it's not to his satisfaction. And we're only on the first track...

On the Preston version, goodness only knows what is up with Morris, for the first ten seconds are as frenzied as Curtis' dancing. When Sumner's guitar comes in (at 0:23, after a fluffed bassline from Hook) it is a relief to hear something familiar and correct. A few crowd members yell appreciation and things settle down. At around 1:20 though, there are hilarious volleys of bum notes from the guitarist, and chaos seems to return for a while. In all, it remains something of a curio recording.

In a review of a 1979 Leeds gig for *Sounds*, Des Moines wrote: "A theatrical sense of timing, controlled improvisation (allowing for apparently arbitrary intro-length), intelligent decibel-variation and good ol' fashioned distortion (unintended or otherwise) are the sum total of Joy Division's secret, as evinced on 'Disorder'."

While it seems a trifle mean-spirited to suggest that the magic of a band can be broken down to just rhythms and volume levels, Moines hits the nail on the head with regards to song structure. The X-factor is much harder, if not impossible, to pin down.

Day Of The Lords
Also recorded: 18/12/79, Les Bains Douches, Paris; 11/1/80, The Paradiso Club, Amsterdam
Versions available on: *Permanent, Heart And Soul, Les Bains Douches 18 December 1979, Refractured*

'Day Of The Lords' is Joy Division at their most heavy-metal sounding. There is something of New Wave Of British Heavy Metal stalwarts Witchfynde, or even Black Sabbath, about the performance across its near-five minutes, with traces of a Warsaw past in the ghostly "Where will it end?" chant. Thankfully it is distinguished from the often pantomime nature of the metal genre by its grinding, relentless four-chord procession. As a modern comparison, the song is more in keeping with the style of guitar music played by the likes of Queens Of The Stone Age (and Kyuss before them), largely based on giant metallic riffs that constantly repeat until a dizzying familiarity is achieved, with heaviness the byword.

After the high-pitched bassline of 'Disorder', encountering 'Day Of The Lords' for the first time (it starts low and gets even lower) only magnifies the demonic sound. Yet, unusually, there are keyboards again. We hear them first at the 54-second mark, spectral and at odds with the low frequencies elsewhere. They owe a certain something to the theremin, a electronic device pioneered in pop in the 1950s by Joe Meek, and often used to eerie effect in sci-fi films of the era. (It will be forever associated with the space race, as Neil Armstrong took an album of theremin recordings to the moon.)

The Paris recording is more telling still. If one song on *Unknown Pleasures* is simply aching to be played live at frightening volumes, 'Day Of The Lords' is it. As each crescendo loops around, the climax of the building noise, only slightly alleviated by Sumner's scratch-scratch-scratch guitar, is met by Curtis almost whispering the last line of his "Where will it end?" question. As the band become more and more worked up, such disturbing restraint has even greater effect.

The four verses offer four different postcards from grim episodes. The first and last take us to a room with bloodsport, sheets on the wall and bodies. The second conjures up an imaginary army of childhood 'friends', and makes the unusually colloquial assertion that withdrawal pain can "do you right in." In the third verse, a car lies at the side of the road, undisturbed, with its windows closed. Curtis recalls talking "in the heat", noting there was "no room for the weak." Have the occupants of the car died? Has there been a suicide or foul play? It's hard to escape a sense of menace.

The critics did not fail to pick up on this. Dave McCullough, writing for *Sounds* in May 1980, noted astutely: "Joy Division's music was always full of spirits and ghosts. They had a mystique that was born of romanticism. Their music often trembled with fear and it couldn't be explained away, that was the great eternal life-spring of any vital and special rock and roll music."

Candidate
Also recorded: 4/6/79, Pennine Sound Studios, Oldham;
13/7/79, The Factory Club, Manchester
Versions available on: *Heart And Soul*

It is indicative of the experimental nature of 'Candidate' that only one official live version exists. Very much a studio piece, it is more a selection of ideas and half-played instrumentation than a fully structured song.

This is not to do it a disservice, as after the long fade-out of the previous track, we are audaciously handed a fade-in for another, one that seems to be a composite of fills and drum rolls. As Curtis' vocal follows the bass (most notably on the line "There's blood on your fingers..."), the listener is taken on an almost abstract journey—as if Curtis is reading a poem over a barren sonic landscape. Shattered guitar parts lend an air of menace, with Hook's bass something like a guide for the listener, slowly treading through this new landscape.

The Hulme version is fairly true to its studio brother, save for the guitar and the rare use of a whammy bar that begins and builds from the 0:34 mark, and then again at 1:28 (although this time minus the whammy). If anything, this version is more succinct, clocking in at just over two minutes, sighing to a close.

In the lyrics Curtis takes the listener on a more personal journey than ever before. Guilt rides across the first of the two verses: "I don't know what... gave me the right to mess with your values, and change wrong to right" stand out as lines that could easily have been written for his wife. Stubbornness is the order of the day in the second verse, but it seems to be down to his personal character, rather than any poetic intent. "I tried to get to you—you treat me like this" reads like a line spoken by a spoilt child. "We're living by your rules—that's all that we know" might be an assertion of discomfort or angst in marriage. The signs are all there.

Described succinctly by Jon Savage in his album review as a "slow, relentless, sucking tension [which] pursues confusion to a dreamlike state," and more obliquely by Dave McCullough in *Sounds* as "...going deeper and further into the sound mix like great black claws searching diabolically into the record player," 'Candidate' is the first full-on assertion that *Unknown Pleasures* is not a straight-ahead rock album, that there is more to hear, albeit far under the surface.

Insight

Also recorded: 31/1/79, BBC Maida Vale Studios, London;
4/3/79, Eden Studios, London; 13/7/79, The Factory Club,
Manchester; 18/12/79, Les Bains Douches, Paris; 11/1/80,
The Paradiso Club, Amsterdam

Versions available on: *Peel Sessions, The Complete BBC
Recordings, Les Bains Douches 18 December 1979, Heart And Soul,
Before And After, Refractured*

Jon Savage: "What did you do on the fourth track of the first
side, where there's that lift...?"

Martin Hannett: "That's a lift."

While there may be no mystery about the sound that
opens 'Insight' (it's the rusty old freight lift in Strawberry),
the rest of the track is not so easily explained.

It's really hard to put the amazing things on 'Insight' into
some order of significance. There's the now familiarly slow
fade-in, unsettling the listener even before anything has
happened. Then there's the lift, the wire doors closing and
opening, taking God knows what to God knows where.
Then, at 1:54, Joy Division riff with synthesizers, forging a
bubbling miasma of sound for nearly 20 seconds that is as
structured as it is freeform, as groove-based as it is freak-out.

As Mick Middles wrote in a live review of a Manchester
gig for *Sounds*, "the music of Joy Division is narrow-minded
and stubborn. It is a tight, dominating noise that is intro-
verted but masterful. An implosion of musical ideas. A
direct result of four people staring at one fixed point. So it
replaces boredom with controlled commitment. It finds its
own perfection."

'Insight' is considered by Jon Savage to be one of the two best tracks on *Unknown Pleasures* (the other follows it). More structured than 'Candidate', it's built around Morris' simple rhythm and uses a menacingly simple bassline that's not always present—listen just after the first keyboard burst for its most effective showing, somewhat distorted and all the better for it. During the prolonged freak-outs, there's a chiming, metallic noise reminiscent of a sitar, as if guitar strings are being rubbed not played—indeed much of the guitar on 'Insight' is about what you think you hear, or what *could* be happening.

The ponderous nature of 'Insight', that fabulous space between the instruments and sense of something resembling peace, makes Curtis' lyrics sound more like poetry than ever, read over an ambient backing track. He is resigned in the opening verse, and mirrors his own dulled sense of dead dreams with the sparkle of youth. In the second verse, someone is addressed directly—"Hey, don't you know you were right?"—and remorse creeps in. The third verse speaks of opportunities lost, so now there is regret too. But by the closing lines, the narrator has come full circle and admits he is "not afraid any more." He has made peace. It's uncertain what this peace now allows him to do, but his tone of voice suggests it might not be enjoyable.

The Parisian take on 'Insight' is slightly different. Stripped of many of the keyboards and synth lines (save for the 'car alarm on helium' of the main section), the group compensate with a moody presence that truly makes the most of the space so missing from the Eden Studios take. With a modern, robust drum sound (partly thanks to the mix), the buzz word here seems to be 'brooding'.

New Dawn Fades

Also recorded: 11/1/80, Paradiso Club, Amsterdam; 2/5/80, Birmingham University

Versions available on: *Still, Heart And Soul, Les Bains Douches 18 December 1979, Refractured*

As Middles notes in his book *From Joy Division To New Order*: "Their music as a whole... with its constant build ups and drop downs, retains a darkly mysterious sexual potency." 'New Dawn Fades' is the most sonically sexy song Joy Division ever recorded.

After a backwards spurt of synth, Morris plays his starkest ever rhythm—still with the echo—and what follows is what many would consider the traditional Joy Division sound, in all its swaying, cloudy, glory. A descending bassline, a mewling, pained, guitar hook and a comparatively sparse drum sound all intertwine beautifully with each another, building to a point where only Curtis' vocals can make the song any more beautiful. Sumner's picking at 1:19 is exquisite, a delicacy on an otherwise pounding song, and climactic too. By the final vocals everything has fused beautifully. As Curtis yells the word "me", Hook plays his high bassline based on the simple pattern Morris' drums, and Sumner interacts with a screech of one of the most mournful guitar lines on the album.

Curtis' lyrics are like a painting. They lurch from the abstraction of lines like "A change of speed, a change of style" at the beginning to the doubting and stark, near-humorous "A loaded gun won't set you free—so you say." If such a line is not already loaded enough (pardon the pun) with hindsight-fuelled sentiment, Curtis screams, in a moment of clarity, "The strain's too much—can't take much more."

On the *Les Bains Douches* version, the fabulous monotony of the bassline is the most instantly noticeable aspect. Something about the relatively low-quality sound recording gives a child-like presence to Curtis' vocals too—at least until he starts singing about "sharing a drink"—and his moping sounds from 3:30 onwards are chilling.

She's Lost Control
Also recorded: 31/1/79, BBC Maida Vale Studios, London; 13/7/79, The Factory Club, Manchester; 19/7/79, Granada TV Studios, Manchester; 15/9/79, BBC 2 Studios, Manchester; 11/1/80, The Paradiso Club, Amsterdam; 28/2/80, The Warehouse venue, Preston; 29/2/80, The Lyceum, London; 3/80, Strawberry Studios, Stockport
Versions available on: Single release, *Peel Sessions*, *The Complete BBC Recordings*, *Substance*, *Permanent*, *Preston 28 February 1980*, *Heart And Soul*, *Before And After*, *Refractured*

'She's Lost Control' deals in deception. Synth drums mingle with natural skins. A bass guitar plays a standard guitar line. A guitar sounds low enough in the mix to be a bass. They could in fact be each other. On top of this confusion, Curtis' vocals are mixed with echoes of themselves until nothing sounds correct. Later that happens to the guitar as well. Parts seem to get higher and higher, then higher still. There is what sounds like a cow-bell—or is that electronic too? And Joy Division accelerate, they go up rather than down, and sound devastating.

There is none of the usual trademark build and drop in evidence here. The band play, then add a layer, then another, and keep adding until the effect is something like too much—especially as Curtis sounds tenser with every line. It starts with drums, then bass, then guitar, then more guitar, then finally vocals, then yet more guitar on top. It's a masterpiece of composition. *Sounds* called it "an r'n'b rooted adventure into primitive ascending emotiveness whereby the song is finally brought to a tense, embittered culmination."

Curtis' opening chant of "There are some things we'll never understand" on the Factory Club recording adds a poignancy to proceedings that makes repeated listening deliciously dark. There is a backing cry of "Control!" from Hook at the climax of each chorus line, and Morris' electro, almost disco trigger sound (and electronic hi-hat), sound more rhythmic and mechanical than even he could have hoped. At 2:51 Curtis bows out with a heavily distorted scream that is truly terrifying, but the rest of the band seem unsure where to go after that—at 3.28 Morris finishes the track, only to start again for a coda.

A well-worked piece of lyrical repetition, 'She's Lost Control' alternates between a girl's condition (Curtis had experienced a girl's epilepsy first hand while working for the job centre, helping the disabled to find work) and the title. The twist, which is almost expected, is that he changes from "She's lost control" to "I've lost control" (and back again).

It's too easy just to say Curtis might have been losing control of his life, either as a result of pressures from Joy Division, his health or marital problems. What 'She's Lost Control' offers is a glimpse of how caring the man was. A line such as

'And she turned to me and took me by the hand" is tender in its delivery: the girl is genuinely turning to Curtis for his advice, placing her trust in him. Later on, he is spooked by her epileptic fit: "And [she] seized up on the floor—I thought she'd die." But by the end (possibly of her life: it's not clear if the character in the story dies, although the girl who influenced the song did), he has realized that he respects her approach to life, saying she "walked upon the edge of no escape and laughed." It seems to be an approach to life with epilepsy that Ian admired, but was also unlikely to emulate.

On the re-recorded version for the single release with 'Atmosphere' in March 1980, the synthetic drums are high in the mix once more. Though metronomic in style, the track has subtle additions and changes. Throughout, there's a synth motif that sounds almost like a cuckoo clock, and the more ephemeral of Morris' cymbals are placed so far out in the mix (right over on the right-hand side) as to be almost in the next track. Curtis is further detached, as is Hook's bass—Martin Hannett seems determined to produce a sense of distance. At 3:56 a string-like section of synth is first employed, right up to the fade, which clearly hails from the same idea pool as the one that thunders behind 'Love Will Tear Us Apart'.

Curtis' lyrical additions on this version are interesting. Aside from the recurring Joy Division theme of darkness, there is talk of living "better with the myths and the lies"—perhaps Curtis has drawn the narrative away from the secondary character towards his own life. It is pure speculation to say he was commenting on his own circumstances, but the shift in emphasis, especially after the gap of 13 months between recording sessions, is hard to ignore.

This is the version of the song that gets a live airing—recorded at the London Lyceum—on the *Heart And Soul* collection. By this time (February 1980) the band have evidently mastered their trade with distinction, performing with an earnestness and a wonderfully economic minimalism that more than justifies the crowd's cheer after just a single smack of the synth cymbal.

On the Preston CD, also from February 1980, the trigger that Morris makes at each bar is almost frightening in the way it sizzles. Aside from this, though, there is little to warrant repeated listening, so crude is the sound recording, save for perhaps a smattering of backing vocals and an extra lyric, bellowed at the close.

Shadowplay

Also recorded: 5/78, Arrow Studios, Manchester; 20/9/78, Granada TV Studios, Manchester; 9/79, *Rock On*, Radio 1 studios; 18/12/79, Les Bains Douches, Paris; 11/1/80, The Paradiso Club, Amsterdam; 28/2/80, The Warehouse venue, Preston; 5/80, Birmingham University

Versions available on: *Still, Permanent, Preston 28 February 1980, Heart And Soul, Les Bains Douches 18 December 1979, Warsaw, Refractured*

Finally we get to hear Stephen Morris using his crash and ride cymbals for something other than just exclamatory touches. His shimmering intro to the track is perhaps the most subtle sound on the whole of *Unknown Pleasures*. As Peter Hook's bass fades in, it becomes clear that Joy Division, for all their studio experiments, oblique literary references and functional style, are a rock band. Nowhere is this clearer than on track seven of their debut album.

U2 simply must have studied this song. The simmering bass style that underpins it has been exploited by them time and time again, and The Edge's reverb-heavy guitar sound seems to have been lifted straight from Sumner's (and Hannett's) toolbox on 'Shadowplay'.

Furiously paced, the song swerves around, careering past the listener and then comes around again. These are the drops and builds that Mick Middles talks about, perfectly exemplified. The bass chugs out one long note, followed by 14 shorter ones and another long one, giving an impression of temporary speed, and Sumner adds one of his familiar, long, stretches of guitar, akin to traffic rushing past. Morris offers only a relatively traditional rock beat, but it helps to underpin the other members, who are often in danger of flying right off the page.

Lyrically 'Shadowplay' is something of a curio. The three brief verses fuse the military obsession of earlier works such as 'No Love Lost' ("As the assassins all grouped in four lines") with the meaningful imagery found in the more effective and powerful "To the centre of the city where all roads meet." Whether the lyric is a work in progress or a fusion of ideas is unclear, but even if the song is only remembered for the cinematic majesty of "To the depths of the ocean where all hopes sank searching for you, moving through the silence without motion, waiting for you, in a room with a window in the corner I found truth," it would still rank high in Curtis' poetic canon.

On the decidedly rough Preston recording there is an oppressive mood which is not helped by continual bursts of feedback (most notable at the opening), and it is difficult to discern whether these are a belligerent gesture to an unruly crowd or a genuine technical malfunction. Sumner's guitar behaves itself at other points, with a real rock solo dominating practically the entire second half of the song.

On the *Les Bains Douches* version, after Curtis yells for a technician to turn the monitors up, we hear a more powerful run-through. Heavier in every way, the song comes alive with some devilishly fast bass drum work from Morris and darkly metallic guitar from Sumner. Curtis is at his peak, confident in every word, never once outdone by the musicians behind him. His cry of "For their own ends!" is cruel and perfect, and the explosion effects never once upstage him. There is a nano-second of silence after the song ends, before the crowd begin to applaud. That nano-second speaks volumes.

Wilderness
Also recorded: 13/7/79, The Factory Club, Manchester; 11/1/80, The Paradiso Club, Amsterdam; 28/2/80, The Warehouse venue, Preston
Versions available on: *Preston 28 February 1980, Heart And Soul, Refractured*

Of all the tracks on their debut album, 'Wilderness' speaks the loudest of the band's Warsaw past. It's very much a tribal-sounding construction from its bass and drums onwards, and something about the chant of the "tears in their eyes" coda is reminiscent of the chorus from 'The Kill', or even 'You're No Good For Me.'

By playing the whole of the neck of his bass, from high to low seemingly in one gull-like swoop, Peter Hook makes this song his own. Morris' frenzied rhythm, made all the more baffling to first-time listeners by the longer echo on the snare catching up with his tom drum, balances the sound well. Sumner's guitar is not fantastic, simply following the latter part of the bass pattern.

'Wilderness' is another of Curtis' great call-and-response lyrics. As a question is asked, it is answered in the latter half of a line. From the opening "I traveled far and wide through many different times" (or on the version from Preston, the more grandiose "where dwell saints and kings"), it's clear that the narrator is a traveller seeking answers. The travels continue throughout, building to the painful conclusion that all he has seen is that "they had tears in their eyes." From a journey that has taken in fantastic sights and religious icons, the overwhelming memory is the crying. From Curtis' raised voice for the repetitive final couplet, this is the image he is trying to leave us with.

In the Factory Club version, Hook's bass is equally impressive on this most thunderous of the recordings. The bassist was no studio slave: even back then he could pull it off in the live arena as well. Listening to the dramatic drum and bass 'solos' from 1:15 onwards, one really appreciates what a strong rhythm section the band had. With no cymbals anywhere on the track, Morris' use of the tom drums is essential to the momentum of the piece, but also no mean physical feat.

Interzone
Also recorded: 5/78, Arrow Studios, Manchester; 13/7/79, The Factory Club, Manchester; 9/79, *Rock On*, Radio 1

studios; 11/1/80, The Paradiso Club, Amsterdam; 28/2/80,
The Warehouse venue, Preston
Versions available on: *Heart And Soul, Warsaw, Preston 28
February 1980, Refractured*

The 16-beat is a rhythm characterized by a double-time
signature on the hi-hat, adding a constant shuffle behind an
otherwise simple beat. 'Interzone' is the first evidence on
Unknown Pleasures of Stephen Morris' breathtaking skills with
it. The track is just as experimental as 'Candidate' but with less
wayward results. We have the beat, wildly faster than anything else on the album (only the opener 'Disorder' comes
close), and a chug of guitar that is as punk as anything on
Unknown Pleasures—it could have been taken from the Pistols.

Then there's the disturbing effect of that piercing scream,
first heard at the six-second mark and recurring every four.
Over a decade later, the Stone Roses would take the stage at
their 'homecoming' Spike Island concert to one of their unreleased instrumentals, a track that bore an uncanny similarity
to the phantom whoops of 'Interzone', except that Morris'
speed was replaced by Reni's fabulous proto-trip hop, and
Hook's rigid plod was usurped by Mani's lolloping loops.

Curtis' demented screams are absent from the live version
from the Factory Club: instead there's a set of deep backing
vocals from Hook. Morris is on fine form, maintaining the
crazed rhythm throughout. At the 1:18 mark Ian Curtis yells,
"Get out!" with a truly manic possession. He is not simply
shouting a lyric; he appears to be actually *living* the line,
exhaling it with an unexpected vigor that shocks, its insis-
tence underlined by the period of silence that follows.

The track's title is borrowed from a William S. Burroughs story, and there is much to absorb in its extended lyric. Curtis' part sees him driven into town by a force, whereas Hook's response is more uncertain, suggesting he has been forced there against his will. In town, both search for friends, but do not find them. The story takes us to a building with 12 windows, and there is a mysterious light which Hook sings was "inserted deep—felt a warmer glow."

Here Curtis is again using his favorite method of taking striking images from imagined scenarios, leaving the listener with only intriguing glimpses of what is going on. "Metallic blue turned red with rust," for instance, tells us nothing about the car save for the colors, yet we feel we know enough, that we understand, from just those six words. It is a sparse, economical way of working and one that is extremely effective when successful.

The subtlety of the studio version, and even the vocals at some points, are lost completely in the crude recording at Preston. Most of the instruments are hidden behind a shield of hi-hat splash, all treble and piercing. Curtis' vocals on the verses are distorted and unintelligible, the spoken middle section is obliterated by feedback, and even Hook's usually reliable bass is lost somewhere in the murk. When the band comes to the sudden, rather ramshackle conclusion, it's almost a relief.

I Remember Nothing
Also recorded: 2/11/79, Winter Gardens, Bournemouth
Version available on: *Heart And Soul*

The longest track on the album, 'I Remember Nothing' couldn't sit anywhere else but mournfully at the end. At high volume, the smash of glass at 48 seconds can still make the unprepared (and even prepared) catch their breath. Ask music fans what was strange about the production of the album, and many will say the breaking glass (or Steve Morris playing drums alone in a cellar/on the roof, depending on which reports you believe).

Yet the glass is not the only significant sound experiment. Yin to the yang of the glass smashing are the light-sabre swooshes of synth. In the first half they spar with, but go on to be coupled with, and finally played alongside the glass sounds towards the end for a far more spectral, fractal feel.

But Sumner's guitar, as minimal as the one-note bassline that counters it, is where the real magic of 'I Remember Nothing' lies. A scratch of a deadened set of strings at 3:46, rhythmic and muted, is prolonged for an age before being released at 4:24 with the memorable, call-and-response blossoming of the two chords, played gristly and grittily in a moment of melody in an otherwise barren soundscape.

This is the section that keeps listeners coming back to the song, the moment a hardened fan will tell the newcomer to listen out for, ears pricked, rising above even the attention-grabbing breaking glass. This subtlety is the real secret behind *Unknown Pleasures* and most of Joy Division's music: funereal and introspective, yet continually subversive and indebted to the spirit and past of punk.

At more than five and a half minutes, the Bournemouth version of the song is woozily experimental, soaked in feed-back above a simple bass. A crowd member is heard to ask

"Have you heard of Joy Division?"; the friend replies in the negative. What the newcomer would have made of the band's most epic, wilfully oblique number is anyone's guess. Great washes of synth loom ominously (sometimes high, sometimes low), and Sumner plays with his guitar, scratching and teasing out feedback until the bizarre end section (commencing 5:09) where all the instruments seem to melt away in yet more screeches of feedback.

The shortest lyric on the whole of *Unknown Pleasures*, 'I Remember Nothing' is a masterpiece of telling snippets, of lines half-formed but fully effective. It starts as something resembling a love song—there's a romantic grandeur in "We were strangers for way too long," as if lovers, meeting for the first time in their thirties, are regretting not encountering one another at 20. But things take a darker turn with the repetition of "violent", a theme that continues. The song is a study of a relationship long since soured, a couple no longer able to communicate. There is awkward, stultifying silence, and the "gaps are enormous."

More alarming is the second verse, which shifts to the third person. "Violent, more violent, his hand cracks the chair" is a line made all the more shocking by the sound of breaking glass, suggesting domination and resigned submission. By the close, the opening line is re-stated, robbed now of all traces of romance. It bears a resemblance to REM's 'Losing My Religion' where a nation was fooled into thinking the song is one of love, when the real sentiment is given away in its bridge—the center of attention is left just "a simple prop to occupy my time."

The effect is scary, and a sombre way to end an already somber album. It is also a great signpost for lyrics yet to flow from Ian Curtis.

Autosuggestion
Also recorded: 2/8/79, Prince Of Wales Conference Centre, YMCA, London; 18/1/80, De Effenaar, Eindhoven
Versions available on: *Earcom 2, Substance, Heart And Soul, Les Bains Douches 18 December 1979, Refractured*

Why was 'Autosuggestion' left off *Unknown Pleasures*? Because 'I Remember Nothing' was on there already. A meandering, lengthy, experiment in much the same vein, 'Autosuggestion' has so many sonic similarities that it would have been almost a duplication. The tempo is identical, and the bassline is as sparse, albeit with three more notes. True, there is more echo on the snare drum, but it's almost to comic effect (check the stuttering finale—surely an indulgence for Hannett?).

The overall feel is one of a work in progress, but the six-minute-plus effort is not without successes: some of the feedback would have sat well in the grooves of a track like 'New Dawn Fades'. The temporary tempo shift around the five-minute mark was a good idea, but in the confines of *Unknown Pleasures*, where a consistent or uniform speed was called for, it may have seemed just too quirky. Whatever, it was surplus to requirements.

Judging by the Eindhoven version, which is two minutes shorter, the track might have been more impressive live. At 1:40 the song erupts, with Curtis' cries of "Say you tried!" mirroring the chaos of the music behind them. Some 25 seconds later all is calm again, a trick repeated at 3:15. Live, the song seems much more complete than in the studio version. Only the lyrics still seem to need work. There are genuinely moving sentiments in lines such as "Everything is kept inside, feel frustration face to face" and their intensity is magnified by the force with which Curtis spits them out. But elsewhere his lines appear to be merely good ideas strung together. On the *Heart And Soul* version there's the clumsy "politicians want more vice," whereas in Eindhoven Curtis omits the line entirely. If, like 'I Remember Nothing', 'Autosuggestion' worked as sonic experimentation for the musicians, here it seems the singer got a chance to test out ideas as well.

The improvisation continued in Bournemouth, with Sumner adding some of the most bizarre guitar parts of his career (just listen to the note-bending at 1:17) on an otherwise composed version that finishes neatly just after the 4:00 mark.

From Safety To Where...?
Available on: *Earcom 2, Substance, Heart And Soul*

While certainly from the same school as 'Autosuggestion', 'From Safety To Where...?' bears a certain resemblance to the monumental 'Love Will Tear Us Apart', at least in the more upbeat moments. The bass is at a familiarly high-pitched level, and something about the fabulously different and discordant guitar hints at the heavy synth washes to come on the single.

The second of two tracks from these sessions to appear on the *Earcom 2* compilation, it's far from being just a studio off-cut. It reveals a Joy Division very much in transition, unsure of whether to be the frenzied, beat-wielding, speed maniacs of 'Interzone' or the bass-heavy, introspective, ponderers of 'I Remember Nothing'. As a result, 'From Safety To Where...?' tries to sit on both stools. As one slower section draws to a close, Curtis gets a second wind and drags his comrades into a chorus (of sorts) at 0:32, with some splendid rattling bottle sounds and glass noise—not smashing, just rattling. Then the down-tempo 'verse' resumes, with Sumner sporadically abusing his guitar again.

This song also offers some of Curtis' simplest, most easily decoded lyrics. He meets the listener in a state of confusion, unsure of where to go but saying he has a ticket to use. Then he reverts to childhood once more, but this time with blurred vision and a scarred memory. In the final verse there's a fatalistic, resigned outlook to proceedings—"Just passing through till we reach the next stage, but just to where—well, it's all been arranged"—before he returns to uncertainty at the close with "Should we move on or stay safely away?".

The Only Mistake
Also recorded: 4/6/79, Pennine Sound Studios, Oldham;
13/7/79, The Factory Club, Manchester
Versions available on: *Still*, *Permanent*, *Heart And Soul*,
'Atmosphere' single release

Another one of Joy Division's rare ascending songs, with an almost summery feel, 'The Only Mistake' brings Morris' skill with the hi-hat cymbals to the fore again. Echoes of Sumner's guitar—in that blissful, almost West Coast, style—can be heard in later Manchester exponents such as James or acts like The Jesus And Mary Chain.

The lyrics center largely around repetition of the title (or a slight variant). There's an element of remorse in the song, but also an arrogance in the narrator saying he has only made one mistake: "a tendency just to take, till the purpose turned sour" leading to "rumours unfound [and] pressures unknown."

It seems odd that a track so wonderfully emotive was left off the album. One can only conclude that the gaps where only drums remain (at 1:08, 2:31 and the outro) were not thought satisfactory and something was still needed here.

The issues had still not been resolved by July 1979, as the hi-hat heavy version recorded at Factory Club still has the drum-only section. Never mind those, though—the attention should be on Curtis' vocals, which move from a childlike whimper (just after the chorus) to a roaring, baritone howl at the peak of each chorus (listen to the great echo in the hall from such monstrous caterwauling, at 3:33).

Exercise One

Also recorded: 31/1/79, BBC Maida Vale Studios, London
Versions available on: *Peel Sessions 1* EP, *Peel Sessions, Still, The Complete BBC Recordings, Heart And Soul, Before And After*

'Exercise One' is a genuinely unsettling track. It's one of the strangest things the band ever committed to tape, at times sounding like the theme to *Rawhide*, at others some ancient Aztec chant. It begins with a Hoover-like echo and builds to a near scream that sounds as if it's calling upon spirits from the deep. It then moves in to a woozy, throbbing riff, egged on by Hook's bulbous bassline. It ends very quickly as well, wrong-footing the listener. Thoroughly bizarre.

The words don't soothe either. In just eight brief lines Curtis touches on drowning, the slowing of a pulse, self-mutilation, dying in a car, crashing in a car and being hospitalized. No judgements are made, merely observations, but these are disturbing in themselves, especially in the context of the music and with hindsight of events.

The Kill
Also recorded: 18/7/77 and 12/77, Pennine Sound Studios, Oldham; 5/78, Arrow Studios, Manchester
Versions available on: *Heart And Soul, Still*

If you strain your ears hard enough, you can just about hear a trace of Elvis on the second Joy Division track to be named 'The Kill'. With its relentless shuffling beat, it's reminiscent of the rhythm section behind the King's 'Marie's The Name (His Latest Flame)', or any 1950s rockabilly exponent you care to mention. It sticks out in their catalog for being so upbeat in a collection of songs largely remembered for doom, long raincoats and dour expressions.

But it's also hard to listen to 'The Kill' and not think Ian Curtis is staring directly at the listener, addressing one person alone. His continual return to the line "through it all I kept my eyes on you" summons up the image of the man on the front of the *NME*, gazing forlornly as he speaks of organizing a death. "Just something I knew I had to do" and "hurts every moment longer" could be cut directly from a typical suicide note. They read like an instruction from a character who has made preparations for his final act, and that's too close to the bone really.

Walked In Line
Also recorded: 5/78, Arrow Studios, Manchester
Versions available on: *Warsaw, Still, Heart And Soul*

That 'Walked In Line' should crop up as almost a footnote to the *Unknown Pleasures* sessions is peculiar. True, it is notable for being almost pedestrian compared to some of the work completed at the time, and Curtis sings in a near monotone voice, low as ever, almost as if it's against his will.

But it's by no means a bad song (the second verse is trimmed by three lines, otherwise the lyric remains the same as the earlier version) and musically, Joy Division are on form. Morris' smooth transition from the frenzy of the main drum part to the marching rhythm that occurs at 1:33 (and again at 2:06) is perfectly executed. Hannett works wonders too—his inspired buzz-saw burst, first heard at 0:33, is almost worth the money alone.

Yet it still sounds like a band tired of playing old songs, even if they're playing it very well. With the possible exception of Curtis, everyone performs perfectly, if perfunctorily. Put simply, other songs were more daring, experimental and ultimately more satisfying.

BBC Television Recordings

Recorded: 9/79, *Something Else* studios, Manchester
Produced by: Recorded live
Available on: *The Complete BBC Recordings* (audio only)

It is continually frustrating that virtually the only way to see Joy Division live is on bootlegs. But from time to time, for a few precious minutes, one can also catch their TV appearances on the BBC's *Something Else* show, still often wheeled out for retrospectives and chart run-downs.

Both clips show a band somewhat nervous and geekish in their performance. To the wider world, those impervious to the magic, they may seem, cruelly, just moments when the singer did that funny dance. Indeed Curtis does flail around, and is compelling to watch, but the other band members too offer glimpses into how very young they were, how their appearance gave them a strong identity, and how proficient they were at their instruments (Morris especially). This last, at least, can be heard on *The Complete BBC Recordings*.

After watching the clips, one is left with a sadness—one that stems from a knowledge there is no more. They really don't make music television like that any more.

Transmission

'Transmission' is structurally fully formed by the time of its TV appearance in September 1979: even Curtis' vocal inflections match the recorded version. Sumner's performance is particularly arresting, playing his part with an improvisational vigor but taking nothing away from the other three. The vocals are particularly well recorded too, with no bleed or distortion even when the loudest, most shrieked, lines are delivered (just after 2:30, for instance).

This version of 'Transmission' bears the hallmarks of a band running through a single they are fully satisfied with, but have yet to grow tired of. Its strength lies in its clarity, due in part to the BBC recording. Without Hannett's studio sheen, the listener can appreciate the nuts and bolts of the tune, and in turn the skills of the performers (especially Morris, who impresses with the fills he simply shrugs off at alternate bars).

She's Lost Control

One can hear instantly the difference Hannett makes to this track if it's listened to alongside the version from the John Peel session on the same CD. Morris' drums have regained their high-pitched thwack, Sumner has his mean guitar line as high as possible in the mix, building up behind the chorus as always. Curtis can almost be visualized losing his cool at 1:35 and 2:47, both times, ironically, when uttering the word "control". His voice is clearer than on *Unknown Pleasures*, and there seems to be a hint of nerves at play. That cannot be said of Sumner, who delivers his ascending guitar at 0:48 with a confidence that is thrilling to hear. Quite why Morris shifts from high tom drum to low at 2:01 is baffling, as the rhythm seems to be lost slightly from that point onwards, but his rolls around the kit at every other point are fascinating enough to distract attention. Finally, Sumner reproduces the whimper of his guitar from the album at the close. The band have got this song well and truly licked.

Was there more...?

In his *From Joy Division To New Order* book, Mick Middles considers the riddle of 'dub' versions of tracks allegedly mixed around the time of *Unknown Pleasures* but not released.

The story goes that when Peter Hook and Chris Hewitt purchased Cargo Studios in Rochdale in the mid-1980s (it would become their Suite 16 studio), they found a stash of tapes. (It's thought these had been kept as some kind of history of work done in the studios.) Hook particularly recalled two tracks: "There were actually some dub mixes of 'Digital' and 'Glass' created by Martin, working alone... When my partner Chris Hewitt finally sold his share [in the studio], he also sold all the tapes that were just sitting around... The dub mixes were gone, lost forever..."

Today Chris Hewitt goes to great lengths to deny these tapes ever existed, but first he sets the scene...

"Me and Hooky were talking about it [Cargo] and we realized it had such great history. Mark E. Smith said that the best records The Fall ever made were recorded in Rochdale. Julian Cope went to record there because John [Brierley, Cargo's engineer] had been engineer for Tractor and Cope had bought [their] *Way We Live, Candle For Judith* and *Tractor* when he was a kid. So we just decided to buy it.

"But that was at a point when New Order were getting bigger and bigger and I was doing a lot of work for Wilson and the Hacienda... I sold my shares... then Hooky did the same, and I think it was then shut down."

But what of the supposed dub mixes of prime-period Joy Division material?

"That's all hokum. We didn't buy Cargo until 1985, and when we bought it, we bought no reels of tape. And John Brierley re-used tape quite often—the same two-inch reel again and again and again.

"The Joy Division stuff that was done at Cargo was 'Atmosphere', 'Digital' and 'Glass'. John Brierley and Tony Wilson worked together at Granada—John was still a camera-man at Granada during the first 12 months of Cargo [1977/78]. Tony tried to talk John into either accepting a low cash fee for the sessions or a percentage points deal on Joy Division sales. John thought the band were crap—he later thought they improved—and opted for a low cash payment.

The studio had not been open long and John needed some cash flow, and who would buy Joy Division anyway if he waited for the longer-term position of a percentage of sales?

"Hardly any clients who came into Cargo bought the two-inch master tapes and Tony didn't, so John would have recorded over the two-inch stuff and when Hooky and I bought Cargo seven or so years later we bought no tapes. There were none left in the building and there are none in John Brierley's attic at his house—we have been through all the reels [and there's] no Joy Division.

"So when we bought the studio, there wouldn't have been any Martin Hannett mixes lying around in boxes anywhere that hadn't seen the light of day. It's bollocks.

"And even if there were some tapes, and we didn't know what was on them, we wouldn't sell them for 50p each [as Hook claimed], just in case!"

Talking to Hewitt, one honestly does not get the impression he is holding anything back. Also, if he, or anyone else, ever did have such tapes, it's very likely they would have been released already, given the enduring interest in all things Joy Division. But the very idea that such studio experimentation once existed but no longer does, makes for a cruelly unachievable ambition for any JD completist.

the art of
saying nothing
"A chance to watch"

"Joy Division were romantic revolutionaries
and the creators of Vampire Rock..."

Tim Burgess, The Charlatans, Manchester

Funny color, black. Just as the four Joy Division lads will forever be remembered in the stark monochrome of photogra-
phers like Pennie Smith or Kevin Cummins, so their arte-
facts—the recorded legacy—will be looked back on and held
up as works of art. And with the *Unknown Pleasures* cover, one
can only really remember the color black.

The Joy Division debut (and indeed all their releases) bears
the stamp of—and contributes to—a distinctive identity that
has become one of the visual signifiers of the era. Factory
Records, for all its foibles, legal confusion and freeform
approach to money management, had an identity that held all
the way through from their early dalliances with club promo-
tion to the biggest of all superclubs, Manchester's Hacienda.

Peter Saville, a design graduate who approached Anthony
Wilson with a view to designing for him before the idea of a
label had even germinated, was never the 'in-house' designer
for Factory Records. (Later designers like Grand Central

Station would make their own mark with their work for Happy Mondays.) But his often stark, sometimes revolutionary sleeves are a vital part of what makes the label stand out.

"Of all the records I've done, *Unknown Pleasures* has this strange iconic status," he says. "A lot of people still cite it as their favorite album and every year there's at least two or three artworks based on it. The myth of Joy Division obviously plays a large part in it, but a lot of it's just down to the sleeve. Stephen *(some reports say Bernard)* found the image in the *Cambridge Encyclopedia Of Astronomy* and it's an absolutely striking picture of a radio wave emitted from a black hole in space. It was perfect for Joy Division; all I had to do was decide where it should go and do the right thing with it."

It certainly is a striking image. Shown in negative and placed in the middle of a vast, black nothingness, with no explanation—or even the traditional band name and title—the radio waves appear frozen and hopeless. (The lack of motion was brought home in a physical sense when the sleeve was textured in the initial print run.) Inside, a stark image of a door (from Ralph Gibson's *The Somnambulist* book and photograph series) occupies the center of one side of the inner sleeve. A visual echo of the door (from the band's rehearsal space), with Curtis scratched into it, would later be immortalized on both the video to 'Love Will Tear Us Apart' and the *Heart And Soul* box set.

Was all sleeve art from the new wave or post punk era so stylized, so stylish? No. One only has to look at the work of Bernard Sumner on the *An Ideal For Living* sleeve to see that. It is by no means a bad cover—the brazen image of a Teutonic youth banging a chest-mounted drum may be contentious—

but there is a crispness and clarity to the sleeve that betrays the do-it-yourself era it emerged from.

The *Earcom 2* sleeve was not designed with the band specifically in mind, as the release was a compilation that reflected the label (Fast Product) rather than the artists. It depicts a white-framed photo of a cliff face, with a climber descending a bright orange and yellow rope, away from the camera. As striking as it is, any sense of real jeopardy on the model's behalf (doubtless the intention) is compromised by the use of not one but four logos at the top edge of the sleeve.

The Electric Circus memorial album, *Short Circuit*, also contained tracks from several artists, but the overall effect of the sleeve is not one of punk mayhem, nor does it bear any signs of the venue. This time the design is in the style of a blueprint, perhaps for a machine or robot. It's clean, almost Kraftwerkian in its execution, and solemn enough so as not stand out too much when placed alongside other Joy Division releases.

With the introduction of Peter Saville on the double seven-inch compilation *A Factory Sample*, the style that Joy Division would be forever associated with was coming together. The two-color (silver and black) sleeve is simple, the main image being of a workman in hearing protection, most likely from the same series as the logo on the Factory club posters and much later label ephemera. Bold black bars on the front and the rear add an air of warning. (These same bars, albeit with yellow between them, would surface all over the Hacienda nightclub in the next decade.)

A sheet of stickers—detailing what happens to "any idiot who eats Hitler's liver," a seaside clown, the protection logo, a urinating man and a doctored comic strip square—were also included in some copies.

Unknown Pleasures apart, the *A Factory Sample* EP is the most effective of the sleeves in providing Joy Division with their visual identity. Dating from the time before they used photography on their sleeves, it is clean and simple, ageless and clinical, and the music is left to speak for itself. It also works very well as both a mission statement for the Factory label and a stepping-off point for all the bands on the release.

For Saville's most overt influence, one has to look again to Kraftwerk. As Nick De Ville observes in his *Album* tome, "Saville acknowledges [Kraftwerk's] *Autobahn* as a seminal influence on his own attitude to design." Kraftwerk themselves had referenced Russian Constructivists like El Lissitzky, and the punks had freely plagiarized the subversive ideas of situationism. Nothing, it seems, is original when you're designing a 12-inch record sleeve.

To put this into context, other sleeve designers of the time were also borrowing from the works of vintage art movements. Barney Bubbles (Colin Fulcher), Malcolm Garrett and Neville Brody were three of the leading artists, and all were aware of the significance of fonts, type faces and the impact of what *wasn't* in the designs they became famous for.

Londoner Bubbles is perhaps the most famous for his distinctively clean approach to design, and he was just as desirous as Saville for some kind of uniformity in his work. His famous 'Blockhead' logo for Ian Dury and Stiff Records— simple text that uses the letters of the word to construct a face—is plain, simple, and without a hint of the superfluous. The influence of Russian constructivism can also be detected.

Malcolm Garrett, who was director of London's Assorted Images company until 1994, designed Buzzcocks' *A Different Kind Of Tension* sleeve in August 1979. It showed a silhouette of the band in a dazzling, yet simple series of triangles and circles, in vivid purple and yellows. While nowhere near as monochrome as *Unknown Pleasures*, the cover gives little away save for a mood, a similar feeling of unease.

Garrett also created the memorable sleeve for Buzzcocks' earlier 'Orgasm Addict' single. The yellow background is in evidence here too, but the spirit of punk is also captured—the reclining female nude, flipped upside down, has an iron for a head, and lips on her bare breasts where her nipples should be. It is a confusing image, full of strange juxtapositions, twisting the Pop Art movement of the 1960s and blatant in its up-yours defiance. It's a totally different mood to the one created by *Unknown Pleasures*, but with its black parallel lines, right angles and stark, crude cut-outs, it is clearly from the same school of succinctness, making a point without words.

Finally, Neville Brody, who today works specifically with fonts but in the early 1980s was at Fetish Records and later at *The Face* magazine. Brody is really more of a typographer, which might seem irrelevant to the Joy Division design story, given the paucity of text on the *Unknown Pleasures* sleeve. But Brody's work with space and form is as much concerned with an elegance and appreciation of line and classicism as Saville, Garrett, Bubbles et al, and would have been influenced by the same fashions and trends.

Saville's influence still lingers today. Coldplay's 2005 album, *X&Y*, sports a cover that could be of the same genetic make-up as *Unknown Pleasures*. A simple series of shapes in the center of the dark cover, with little given away and no words to help the viewer—you are practically describing Joy Division's debut to someone who has never seen it.

American acts too have drawn on the minimalism of post-punk sleeves. Green Day's *American Idiot* (2004) cover has a clenched fist with a grenade raised in the air, in basic cartoon form. While it hints at humor and is a long way from the spartan solemnity of Factory, the simple color scheme and bold typeface are certainly in keeping with the same influences—particularly the Russian ones—that Saville and his like held dear.

Similar sparseness is evident on The Killers' *Hot Fuss* (2004) which shows, in photo form, a selection of Japanese high-rise buildings. The similarity between this and the 12-inch version of Joy Division's 'Transmission' single is uncanny. Although one is taken at night and the other at dusk, the evocative neon lights, slightly blurred in each shot, set the mood for the epic music in both packages.

But of all the distinctive designers whose work became one of the hallmarks of the post-punk era, it is Peter Saville who has made the most impact. His work with Joy Division signalled the start of an era, and its influence spread far outside of the Factory stable. Like the music it contains, the sleeve of *Unknown Pleasures* is striking, arresting and memorable, signifying and representing so much while remaining undated and timeless more than 25 years after its creation amid shifting fashions, artistic ideals and musical boundaries.

location and identity

"To the centre of the city where all roads meet"

"Peter Hook's always been a great guy. I can remember me
and my mate going to the Deeply Vale Festival in 1978, and
my mate was hitching on the way back, and Hooky stopped
and gave him a lift—he'd just come off stage!
He's one of the boys, Hooky, a really nice guy"

Ian Brown, singer and former Stone Rose, Manchester

"We never were part of the music industry because we were
on a little independent label up in Manchester. We never,
ever had any contact with the music industry. Until we went
off and did our solo projects. Oh, and when New Order got
signed to London."

Bernard Sumner has some insightful theories into why his
band(s) endured through the shifting fashions of the 1970s
and 1980s. He still seems content that his band stayed loyal
to Factory for so long, not least because their success early on
had a lot to do with the shield the label provided from the
pressures of the industry. And he is realistic enough to know
that in the end it always comes down to business.

"You're an investment. That's the way it works, you're
just simply an investment. The company either are or are
not passionate about music. I understand that, though. I
understand that they've got to run a business, they've got

people to employ, bills to pay. They've got money to make. That's the way capitalist society works. Fortunately, we were insulated from that and allowed to develop in our own daft little way. Which was a very good thing for Joy Division. There weren't the pressures of delivering a commercial single or a commercial video, or you must play whatever territory. We were allowed to be like childish brats for most of our twenties."

One has to wonder though: if things had been different and Joy Division had gone down to London, how different would they have been? What exactly set the band apart, outside of their music? Can their essence be found in their image, that functional, working-class style that suited them so well?

Dave McCullough, writing in *Sounds* in August 1979, thought so, and picked up on the band's approach to image. "Their dress is somewhere between a factory-worker's eye for the practical and early and middle period Buzzcocks' eye for the proletarian chic, somewhere between the contrived and the non-contrived... perhaps a representation in clothes of the truth about Joy Division."

Mick Middles, however, isn't so sure.

"It's a funny one that you know, because to me Ian Curtis dressed like a civil servant, and he *was* a civil servant. At the time, a lot of people seemed to dress like him, so he was very unfashionable in that respect. But that kind of became their image, didn't it?"

Joy Division's identity was established—and fixed in time forever—by Kevin Cummins' famous January 1979 *NME* cover shot (recently reproduced in *Mojo*). In it, Curtis leans against a wall in his military overcoat, Red Star badge on his lapel, smoking a cigarette and gazing out at us.

"And there was that other cover [story] that Paul Morley did," Middles adds, "with the words 'Joy Division come marching into town', and it looked like they'd just come from the office. It was quite a big statement. I kind of think it happened by accident. I mean, Hooky really, he belonged in a heavy metal band, didn't he? He still does!"

Bernard Sumner insists their image wasn't planned. "Absolutely not. We're not, in any shape or form, strategists. We've always kind of stumbled our way along, you know? Our aim really was to create lives for ourselves where we just had a good time. And the by-product of having a good time was to make music, because you were happy. If you're happy and you're having a good time you enjoy making music."

Read no further if you want to think the whole Joy Division ethic was based on a life of seclusion and ascetic contemplation. "I remember speaking to Karl from Kraftwerk," Sumner recalls, "and he said: 'Oh, I saw you play in Düsseldorf, you were really pissed on stage, and the show was terrible. Why did you do that?' I said: 'Well, the purpose of doing the show was so that I could get pissed.' I suppose it was just an anarchistic lifestyle, really."

As live performers, Joy Division, perhaps as a consequence of 95 per cent of their fans never having seen them play, remain ingrained in our mind's eye as four, small-framed, men performing on *Something Else* or *Granada Reports*. Or if we're lucky, from a bootleg DVD, perhaps recorded at a venue like Bowdon Vale Youth Club, where someone had snuck a camera in—shaky, grainy and badly lit. They are all poignant images, not least because of Curtis' magnetism on stage and his later suicide, but there is also something about the music, the way that music was packaged, and the era from which it sprang, that makes it indelible.

Ultimately the shadowy men will be remembered too as Mancunians. Jon Savage (himself a Manc) wrote in the *Melody Maker* of late July 1979, musing on the significance of location in *Unknown Pleasures*. "[Joy Division's] themes… are one perfect reflection of Manchester's dark spaces and empty places, endless sodium lights and hidden semis seen from a speeding car, vacant industrial sites—the endless detritus of the 19th century—seen gaping like rotting teeth from an orange bus." Not the prettiest of pictures but a memorable one, and if soundtracked correctly, one remembered forever.

Crispy Ambulance's Alan Hempstall remembers a spirit emerging in the city at the time. "Joy Division couldn't give a flying fuck. *Really* couldn't give a flying fuck. Everyone was really down to earth. Everybody was doing it for the love of it really. Who cared if we made some money? We were playing music and we enjoyed it. Nobody was in any way starry or above themselves. That was one of the nice things about it all."

Manchester bands seemed to help one another then. Hempstall again: "Apparently the whole band [Joy Division] and Rob [Gretton] came to see us at the Band On The Wall. This would have been mid-'78. They'd been rehearsing, they wanted to stay out and have a few beers. It just so happened that we were on the bill. About six months after that, Joy Division played at The Factory club, and the day after that I was in Virgin Records and in walked Bernard. So I collared him and we were shooting the breeze, and he asked me what I did. I told him I was in a band but I didn't expect him to have heard of us. I was floored when he said they'd been to see us six months earlier. He was in the audience and I didn't even notice. I asked him which gig it was, he described it, and it was probably the worst gig of the first 12 months of our career, by a long mile. Yet within another three months we were on the bill with them. It was about the time *Unknown Pleasures* came out, about July '79, when we supported them at The Factory club."

In an intriguing footnote to this spirit of togetherness in the young Manchester music scene, Hempstall remembers a gig at the Derby Hall in Bury when he was asked to stand in for an ailing Ian Curtis. (This collaboration was the second Joy Division gig that evening.)

"I read somewhere that Steve Morris said they should never have done that gig. I'm inclined to agree with him: I don't know what made them do it, and I don't know what made them push to do two gigs in a night. Ian was ill: I think he had a fit onstage. It was either The Stranglers or Robert Fripp's band they were supporting, and then they had to do a gig at the Derby Hall afterwards. Twice in a night—working the guy too hard! But hindsight's a marvelous thing isn't it? They didn't want to disappoint the fans.

"I just got a phone call, I was told Ian was ill—I didn't realise at the time. I knew Ian as a friend, I didn't know any of the troubled side at all. He was always good fun when I was with him. The whole band were, they were just Salford lads.

"So Bernard just said: 'Look, Ian's ill, could you stand in for him?' I turned up to the gig and was most surprised to find Ian there. He said: 'Oh, I don't feel too good—I'll do a couple of slow ones.' I found out we were going to do a shortened set, and it was going to be buttressed against Section 25's. I was like a kid in a sweet shop, because they asked me to pick two songs that I liked. Great. So I picked 'Digital', which was always a favorite, and 'Love Will Tear Us Apart'. The latter wasn't even out then, but I'd heard the John Peel demo which had been broadcast in January, and I'd been to the recording session for the single. So I knew the words off by heart.

"The Minny Pops from Holland came on first and did a full 45-minute set. Then Section 25 came on, and their last number was 'Girls Don't Count.' At that point me, Bernard, Steve and Hooky came on stage, with Simon Topping from A Certain Ratio, and we all went into that song as a kind of supergroup. Simon and I were doing backing vocals to Larry [Cassidy] from Section 25's lead. No one knew what was going on. When that song finished, Larry, Simon and the rest of Section 25 left the stage, leaving me and three of Joy Division.

"I did 'Digital' and 'Love Will Tear Us Apart', then Ian came on and did 'Decades' and 'The Eternal'. He then left the stage. Then I came back on with Larry and Simon, and we did 'Sister Ray' with Larry on lead, and me and Simon doing backing vocals. By this time, no one knew what the fuck was going on. The whole thing, after Section 25 came on to 'Sister Ray', was about 30-35 minutes. The crowd felt short-changed."

Any idealistic notion of a greater Manchester musical oneness clearly didn't extend as far as the aggrieved audience.

"Just as we were leaving the stage, someone picked up a bottle and threw it. The venue, an old town hall, had a big chandelier and the bottle hit it square on, and as we left the stage we were showered with shards of crystal glass. Tony Wilson and Alan Erasmus ushered us into this dressing room, and locked the door. The next thing we knew was all these beer bottles smashing against the dressing room door..."

In the 25-plus years since Joy Division first found fame, the city of Manchester has continued to give the world landmark bands. The Smiths, a fabulous melting pot of rockabilly, rock 'n' roll and modern blues, found fame in the mid 1980s, singer Morrissey's literary savvy injecting their lyrics with a cynicism but overlooked romanticism that would see them held up as the last great guitar band of the age.

Following them, The Stone Roses and Happy Mondays brought the rougher edges of the city into sharper focus—real people with real problems making real music. Great albums were made (*The Stone Roses* remains a much loved classic, but Happy Mondays' *Pills, Thrills And Bellyaches* actually stands up better). At various points, both bands were also held up as the last great guitar band of the age.

In the 1990s Oasis, a five-piece from the suburb of Burnage, took the whole world by storm with more guitar music, spearheading the Britpop movement while acting as a grittier counter to the cool Blur set in the south. They offered the realness of the Mondays and musical cap-doffing of the Roses, but with a songwriting ability in debt to the likes of Johnny Marr (Smiths) and Squire/Brown (Stone Roses).

Today the city still keeps giving the world great bands. Doves and Elbow make giant, lurching, anthemic, rock songs that come from the same school as those from the Gallagher pen, but also draw on the same well of existential angst and catharsis that had fuelled Curtis and crew 25 years earlier. Yet the music of the city has not so much come full circle as drawn from past successes before creating something both new and familiar. And if you like, that's really what the short story of Joy Division was all about anyway.

a turn for the worse

"The myths and the lies"

"I never picked up on the doom and gloom. It was ironic, because The Fall were supposed to be the ones with the sense of humor, and then you met them and they were right miserable bastards! And Joy Division were the ones having all the fun. They were the ones who were most likely to give you a wedgie as you bent over. The Fall were more likely to slag off your clothes or your choice of music"

Alan Hempstall, Crispy Ambulance singer, Chorlton

The most obvious signs that Joy Division existed in a very different era to today come when one looks at the comparatively scant promotional activity the band had to carry out for the release of *Unknown Pleasures*. In June 1979, they were booked to do a session for Piccadilly Radio in Manchester, which was recorded at Pennine Sound studios in Oldham. Remarkably, only one track ('Candidate') from the new album was aired. The later single 'Atmosphere' appeared (as 'Chance'), and the other three tracks would either make their way on to their second album *Closer*, or languish in the vaults—perhaps lending credence to the idea that their minds were already racing ahead.

A flurry of TV activity followed—well, two appearances. On 20 July the public were treated to an airing of 'She's Lost

Control' (a track much more in keeping with the record they were actually promoting) on Granada TV's *What's On*. This was a regional news and listings programme for the north west of England that had Anthony Wilson as chief band booker. (These musical slots ran after the news in the early evening, and are fondly remembered for slotting Curtis and his manic dancing in among stories of local interest.) On this occasion Joy Division were the last item on the show and the song—played live in the studio—was cut short at 2:30. The closing credits were also superimposed over their performance and an announcement was made about the next show, which is probably why this clip is so rarely aired.

Two months later, on 15 September, Joy Division made their only national TV appearance—on *Something Else* (a BBC2 show that mixed youth issues with live music) playing 'She's Lost Control' again and 'Transmission'. There was also an interview with Stephen Morris and Anthony Wilson—no prizes for guessing who did most of the talking.

Between these two broadcasts, the band performed across the country, but mainly divided their time between London and Manchester. On 27 July they returned north for a festival called Stuff The Superstars at the Mayflower venue. Mick Middles remembers it fondly.

"The Mayflower was a bit like the [Electric] Circus—a crumbly old venue, much loved. [Stuff The Superstars] was an all-day festival put on by *City Fun* magazine, the local rag. It was fantastic—you had all these great bands on, and some dodgy ones too. I seem to remember Joy Division played at midday. I think it finished with The Distractions, one of the greatest lost bands in Manchester history. The reason they were important was because they supported Joy Division a lot—they were like the light Joy Division. There was a very important meeting at Island when they had to decide whether to drop U2 or The Distractions. But that day was great."

By this time Joy Division had improved dramatically as live performers. One only needs to listen to a live bootleg from either end of that period to fully appreciate just what working with Hannett and continual gigging had done for their playing and their sound. Middles remembers a distinct change in the band as performers. "By their own admission Joy Division were good because they were bad musicians, in a way. But they improved unbelievably, in a small period of time. I don't think I've ever seen a band improve as rapidly."

"Joy Division came to the fore when they shelved the Warsaw tag and got with Factory," recalls Crispy Ambulance's Alan Hempstall, "and from their first 12" single, their sound didn't half change."

Middles claims to have seen the band more than most, and as he details in his writings, the Joy Division live experience was distinctly variable. "I saw them probably about 16 or 17 times, mainly in Manchester, but a few in London as well. They were always slightly different in London.

"I saw some really bad [gigs] too. I think the most famous really bad one was at the New Osborne Club, round the corner from the Electric Circus, and it was the night Iggy Pop went to the gig. They played with A Certain Ratio and Section 25—they were at their peak at that point, but there was loads of pressure on them, but they just did not perform at all. I think that was the biggest audience they ever had in Manchester and probably the worst gig they played there."

Joy Division, for all their status and burgeoning respect, were known for turning in terrible gigs at the most inopportune moments. There are many theories as to why this was, but the most accurate is probably simply luck. After all, many people interviewed for this book recalled the band as amongst the greatest they ever saw. Middles falls into this category.

"My opinion is that Ian was a performer in the sense that he would wind the band up. If he was on form the band was on form. If not, the band could be a bit sloppy. He just had to twitch and then suddenly... But if he wasn't feeling well that night, maybe that was it. I do think a lot depended on him and his mood. Not that he was a musician, I just think his presence had that effect.

"He was very volatile, which is probably why they were volatile in their approach to the gigs. If they were on a downer it showed, which is very honest. You never quite knew what you were going to get with them, but if you got them at their best, they were the best band I've ever seen. Without any question."

Joy Division were also members of a cooperative organisation called the Manchester Musician's Collective. "They were a weird bunch," recalls Alan Hempstall. "It was run by a couple of hippies, who used to gather every Monday night in a pub on Deansgate called The Sawyers Arms. Crispy Ambulance had been going for about a year and in January 1979 we decided we needed to be part of this union, to get a regular gig. Their regular venue was the Band On The Wall, every Sunday night. I'll never forget the first meeting I turned up at. The Fall were sat in one corner, Joy Division in the other, a whole host of other smaller bands, and us, all chatting together. So as much as The Fall and Joy Division professed to not like one another—I mean, they were definitely different sides of the tracks—there they both were, opposite sides of the same table."

Curtis remembered Joy Division's time in the Collective fondly when talking to a local Manchester newspaper. "The Collective was a really good thing for Joy Division. It gave us somewhere to play, we met other musicians, talked, swapped ideas. Also it gave us a chance to experiment in front of people. We were allowed to take risks—the Collective isn't about music that needs to draw an audience."

Away from the city, the largest ever Joy Division headline gig took place on 26 October at the Electric Ballroom in London, in front of 1,200 people, with support from The Distractions and A Certain Ratio. It seems strange given the interest in the band today that a fairly middling London venue would be the biggest that Joy Division would headline, but even together the three developing acts simply weren't a big attraction in a city spoiled for choice when it came to live music. But in one way the relative intimacy of these smaller gigs worked in their favor, helping to create a more personal bond with their audience.

"[Anthony] Wilson doesn't agree with me," says Mick Middles, "but I don't think Ian could have become a Bono. Or an international rock star. And I don't think Joy Division could have. I might be wrong, but as it happens they never got the chance…"

In his review of Joy Division that day Adrian Thrills wrote in *NME*: "Each instrument retains a crisp, distinctive identity: the overloaded, distorted Rickenbacker bass of Peter Hook;

Albrecht's incisive guitar figures; the primal, syndrum-embellished *thwack* of Steve Morris; and the gruff intensity of Curtis's vocals.

"Fellow Mancunians Buzzcocks are a brave band indeed to take Joy Division on their forthcoming tour as main support. I can think of very few groups who are capable of following them."

The Buzzcocks support tour of October and November saw Joy Division play to some of the biggest halls, if not audiences they could call their own, in their short career. Depending on who you talk to, the Buzzcocks shows were either stolen completely by Joy Division, or vice versa. Mick Middles was assigned to review one of the dates.

"If you ask Steve Diggle [Buzzcocks] he'll say Buzzcocks blew them [Joy Division] off the stage. They were further advanced in terms of musicianship. But Joy Division were better than them when they hit their peaks. I saw the two [Manchester] Apollo gigs and one in Leeds. But at Leeds I was only allowed to write about Buzzcocks. Buzzcocks and [their manager] Richard Boon were paranoid, and I should know, because he actually drove me there *after* Joy Division played! It was like that, there was that kind of tension between them. You really wouldn't want Joy Division, at that point, to be your support band.

"But having said that, most people who went to those gigs went to see Buzzcocks. They were great. Everyone said to me that they got on fine. There were japes, but that was about it."

Japes? Japes?? This is Joy Division, not rock 'n' roll! But as Pat Gilbert confirmed in his piece on the tour in *Mojo* magazine in 2004, "There were lots of hi-jinks. In Cardiff, the hotel bar shut at 2am, so the roadies prised off the metal grilles and handed out free beer, the night ending in a huge drunken cushion fight between main act and support. In Guildford, Joy Division surpassed themselves by removing the strip lights from the gents' toilets and smearing the taps and light switches with excrement."

With the tour such a hot ticket, such japery can be taken as a sign that the two bands were comfortable in each other's presence and playing at the top of their game. Press reports from the tour were glowing.

"'She's Lost Control' and 'Transmission' carried the impact of mini epics. Their heavily stylised claustrophobia might eventually constrict them, but for the present it's exciting, and their expand [sic] on it in the future should be worth watching," wrote Chris Bohn in *NME*.

"Instead of punters slashing their wrists, there were people dancing. Instead of dirges, there were experiments with varying speeds within one song. The only image is non-image, uniformity of clothing... It's music that washes over you, music to surrender to," said *Penny Kiley in Melody Maker.*

Both of the Manchester dates (27 and 28 October) on the tour were filmed for posterity, and segments of the shows can be found on the *Here Are The Young Men* video, which was released through Factory's film division, Ikon.

It was around this time that Ian Curtis became romantically involved with a beautiful, dark-haired Belgian girl named Annik Honoré, a fan of the band. There is no doubt that the affair happened, because eventually it became public knowledge and has been long-since documented by band and fans alike. When the affair started isn't known—Joy Division went to Brussels on 16 October for the first ever

Factory foreign trip, but Honoré was working at the Belgian Embassy in London, so their paths may have crossed earlier.

The involvement with Honoré is a difficult one to accept for anyone wishing to see Curtis as some kind of angelic, virtuous character in the Joy Division story. True, he chose to live his life in the arena of rock 'n' roll, but that was only half the story. Away from the band Curtis had a family, and even a full time job as a civil servant for much of the band's life, and divorce was far from as common as it is today. Add to this his troubles with epilepsy, and certain lines and certain cries on record become all the more heart-rending.

Particularly painful with regards to Curtis' home life is 'Love Will Tear Us Apart,' recorded initially for the second John Peel session (broadcast on 10 December but recorded two weeks earlier). Now regarded as a modern classic, it charts the demise of a relationship, one destroyed by love. It's an odd sentiment, but becomes crystal clear when you look at the circumstances under which it was written, back in August 1979. Singer Paul Young, who later covered the track on his UK chart-topping *No Parlez* debut album (1983), remembered in *Mojo*: "Once you see the lyrics written down, you realise how powerful they are and how they could be reinterpreted as a soul song." The song would become the defining Joy Division moment to many, but like 'Transmission' it would not make it on to a Joy Division album (compilations aside).

After touring Europe in the early months of 1980, Joy Division returned to Britain to find a country more than ready to check them out live, bootleg their performances and swoon over the photography on the covers of the music press. The band's next move, however, was to take advantage of the freedom offered by their Factory deal to donate the as-yet unreleased 'Atmosphere' and 'Dead Souls' tracks to a French art label called Sordide Sentimental, to be part of an ongoing series. The record was released in March in a limited run of 1,578 copies, under the name 'Licht Und Blindheit' ('Light And Blindness').

Rob Gretton, speaking to the *NME* at the time, humorously recalled the move. "We had a pleading letter from Jean-Pierre Whatsit, and we agreed 'cos it's interesting to see how different people handle different aspects. There are no restrictions from Factory on this sort of thing."

Also in March, the band entered Britannia Row studios in London to record what was to become their second (and final) album, *Closer*, again working with producer Martin Hannett. The punk and fury of *Unknown Pleasures* were replaced with an eerie solemnity, and washes of synthesizers blossomed where before they had only tentatively peeked out from the instrumentation. Ian Curtis' lyrics too moved to a new level, but were more pointed, darker, and without doubt fuelled by his increasingly shaky marriage and medical situation.

Throughout April, Joy Division, keen to please their growing fanbase, gigged hard. It was not uncommon for Curtis to suffer epileptic fits on stage, leading to a brief period of rest. This was practically forced upon him by a potentially fatal overdose of his medication on 7 April. In early May, after selected cancellations in Scotland and with their first visit to America just days away, the band played what was to be their last gig, at Birmingham University. It contained the only live performance by Joy Division of the song 'Ceremony', then still a work in progress.

On 18 May 1980, after an evening spent listening to Iggy Pop and watching Werner Herzog movies, Ian Curtis, aged 23, hanged himself in the home he still shared with his wife. He is greatly missed.

Factory pushed on. Few begrudged them the posthumous release of *Closer*, which sold well, or the 'Love Will Tear Us Apart' single which climbed to number 13 in the UK charts, aided by industrial action cancelling *Top Of The Pops*. (This meant the usual mainstream pop didn't receive its customary weekly promotional boost from the country's most influential—and at that time almost the only—TV music show.) Factory even pushed out a single release for 'Atmosphere' in September, which was perhaps pushing it a touch.

In 1981 the catch-all *Still* double album was released, which featured the final Birmingham gig and off-cuts from the *Closer* sessions. Five thousand copies were released in a gray, hessian, double sleeve with a white ribbon down the centre, as if to mark the page. Other Joy Division releases from outside their lifespan include a BBC Sessions compilation, the exhaustive and well put together *Heart And Soul* box set, the *Permanent* best of and the *Substance* compilation, along with reissues of 'Love Will Tear Us Apart' and 'Atmosphere'. Also issued were CDs of the band as Warsaw, and live recordings from Preston and Eindhoven. The bootleg scene is, of course, a law unto itself.

After the death of Ian Curtis, it seems even those closest to Joy Division were surprised when the other three members decided to continue as New Order. The Fall's Marc Riley remembers their first gig: "I remember getting a call asking if I wanted to go see Joy Division, but without Ian Curtis, at The Beach Club—a weird little, rickety old place on Shoe Hill at the back of Manchester. That was the first gig that they did. I saw them, and they were just finding their feet. It was a strange feeling anyway, because it was the same three guys, without Ian."

That was until they recruited Stephen Morris' girlfriend, Gillian Gilbert (born 27 January 1961, in Manchester), on keyboards and guitar. There was a slight overlap where both bands coexisted, then New Order (as the new band became) released 'Ceremony' as their first single the following year— a song they had written in their previous incarnation. The album it came from, *Movement*, was largely well received, even if it took some time for hardened Joy Division fans to get used to Sumner on vocals.

But it was with 1983's *Power, Corruption And Lies* that the group really started to cut their historical ties and make music that was purely New Order, aided and abetted by a burgeoning love of new technology. With Sumner no match for Curtis as a lyricist, the cerebral nature of much of Joy Division's work was replaced by a blank canvas. Yet though Sumner was often described as saying nothing with his lyrics, he was still saying enough to get emotion across to a listener.

Then there was the small matter of a song called 'Blue Monday', nowadays referred to by Peter Hook as 'Fucking Blue Monday' because of the way public demand for it has come to dominate their musical life. A 12-inch only single (it became the biggest ever seller in that format), it was a marvelous and fresh-sounding electronic dance song, with traces of Joy Division lingering in the dispassionate delivery of lines like "How does it feel, to treat me like you do?"

New Order have often argued that they didn't even 'write' the song, that it fell together from a demo of a piece of new equipment, that the first time it was played it was when no members of the band were even on stage, and other such distancing tactics. But it remains a vital record, even outside the arena of international dance music, and it still excites today, regardless of how many times you've heard it before.

Its global success led them to work with New York dance producer Arthur Baker for their epic 'Confusion' and 'Thieves Like Us' singles in 1983 and 1984 respectively, but they still remained loyal to their beloved Manchester, and to the Factory label in particular.

A couple of mixed years followed: the *Low Life* album (1985) was perceived by some as their best, but experimentation with other producers left many cold. 1986's *Brotherhood* was more of the same. Somewhat bizarrely, in 1988 the group allowed Quincy Jones to remix 'Blue Monday' which, although it produced a chart success, remains a puzzling move. Remixes are de rigueur in dance circles, but with the original a stirring example of both period and timeless production, was there really any need to give it a fashionable spin for the masses of the day?

In 1989 the band went to Ibiza to record the *Technique* album. As with many bands who go abroad to record, the result was infused with local influences, in this case the dance rhythms and sunshine of the island. Fans seemed to pick up on this, sending the 'Fine Time' single high into the charts.

Ask anyone about the links between football and music and 1990's England World Cup anthem, 'World In Motion', written by New Order and performed with the England squad of the time, will come up in conversation. A number one in their home territory, the song was likeable enough, but with a video showing the four members clowning around with the footballers and assorted comedians of the time, it would probably leave most Joy Division fans cold.

The 1990s were interesting, if sporadic times for New Order. Now signed to London Records after the demise of the first Factory incarnation, they released *Republic* in 1993, which contained three massively memorable singles ('Ruined In A Day', 'Regret' and 'World'), but offered little else to fans hungry for a more consistent, high quality, album. There were best ofs, remix collections and BBC recordings, but the closest fans got to new material were the collaborations or solo projects, some of which were brilliant.

Sumner joined the flexible line-up of Electronic with Johnny Marr (late of The Smiths), finding success with songs co-written with the Pet Shop Boys. Hook continued to plough his heavy rock furrow with acts like Monaco and Revenge. The other two wittily formed The Other Two, releasing the lukewarm *The Other Two And You* (1993) and the far stronger *Superhighways* (1999).

The new millennium finds New Order in a lofty position. They have released two albums—*Get Ready* (2001) and *Waiting For The Sirens' Call* (2005)—but these have been far from their best work. Too full of Sumner's now all-too-vacant lyrics, they also find the band honed into more of a standard rock band. (Gilbert left in 2000, and an anonymous-sounding second guitarist—Phil Cunningham, ex-Marion—was brought in two years later to help in the live arena.)

The band still play Joy Division material live, as they have at various points of their career. Their shows at the Glastonbury and O2 London Wireless festivals of 2005 saw them run through not one but four numbers across the two nights, with Sumner taking vocal duties. Reception has been cold, especially from older fans, but there is still something to be said about seeing a younger generation avidly lapping up the old material.

Sumner has also worked with dance artists/DJs The Chemical Brothers, providing vocals for their 'Out Of Control' single (1999), a romp through the big beat with which the duo made their name, laced with Sumner's monotone wit. But New Order have always experimented, for better or worse, and this again harks back to the quote about Joy Division heads being years ahead of their bodies. It's tempting to consider that, had Curtis lived to see the many avenues of music New Order went on to explore, he might well have embraced such endeavors himself. But until someone remixes some old Joy Division vocal tracks, we'll just have to imagine. And the greater part of this writer hopes that day never comes.

the legacy

"Looking for some friends of mine"

"I think that intimacy is a big part of their legend. They would have lost something if they'd gone on to be a bigger band. I don't see how they could have maintained that. They were a big band in a small capsule. It certainly made it more intense"

Mick Middles,

Joy Division, Factory Records and New Order biographer, Stockport

The Joy Division sound is everywhere today, but perhaps most interesting is the band's influence on groups who were their contemporaries, or who followed swiftly in their wake.

U2, arguably the world's biggest band and certainly one of the most longstanding (having formed roughly around the same time as Joy Division), might not seem an obvious comparison. True, the first half of their recorded output hints at more US-based influences (*The Joshua Tree* says it all), but from *Achtung Baby* onwards the band dynamic seemed to spin on its axis. Bass became more prominent. Guitar lines, once stadium-sized and bombastic, were now higher in pitch, sometimes shrill, and ever simpler (albeit still stadium-sized). Yet U2 started as a punk band, and the parallels between the two bands—as with many punk and post-punk outfits of the era—are strong.

But the kinship continued long after punk and post-punk fizzled out. On *Boy*, Bono dedicates the track 'A Day Without Me' to Ian Curtis, although it could just as easily be 'inspired by'. Visually there are parallels as well. Obviously fashions of the time had a big hand in the way the two bands were portrayed, but the way they were documented too was uncanny. Photographer Anton Corbijn, who has pretty much been photographer in residence for U2 since their *WAR* album of 1983, has directed videos, albeit posthumously, for Joy Division ('Atmosphere', 1988). There is a solemnity, too, in the man's work that seems now to go hand in hand with the memory of Joy Division.

The rock cliché of four boys forming a band to get out of whatever crap job/poverty/humdrum town they find themselves in, or address whatever social injustices they see, holds true worldwide. Joy Division simply didn't get as far as U2. It's pushing the comparison to say that they would have opened Popmart or telephoned Salman Rushdie live from the stage, but the scope was always there. Besides, they were busy becoming New Order.

Across the Atlantic, Interpol—modern-day alternative Goths—have largely been the ones carrying the Joy Division flame. Singer Paul Banks has the nasal whine of Curtis at his highest range, and the frenzy of Sam Fogarino's drums is Stephen Morris (Joy Division version) for the modern age. Some say Interpol borrow rather too heavily, but their sound is robust enough, and filtered with just the right amount of a New York dance/rock club vibe to give them their own identity. Their look is utilitarian as well, which helps you compare if you catch them live.

Goth is something of a dirty word, especially when used in relation to Joy Division. Perennially unfashionable, members of the movement more commonly known for a fascination with the darker side of existence often cross over into the Joy Division fanbase. Of course, a genuine fan is exactly that, but something about seeing the band's name listed on a poster or flyer for a club alongside the likes of The Sisters Of Mercy, Alien Sex Fiend or All About Eve seems wrong.

With Joy Division, there was no element of them 'dressing up', of them putting on a mask, specifically not on *Unknown Pleasures*. The music is certainly dark in tone, and lyrically there are grand, sweeping statements about death, but it is a different kind of misery. It would be insulting to every Goth to say their feelings weren't genuine, but the themes touched upon in a song like 'She's Lost Control' run far deeper into the human psyche than an upside-down crucifix or pentagram ever could.

In recent years the rhythms of Joy Division, and more particularly Stephen Morris, have become inspirational to a newer generation of groups who fuse elements of both club and rock culture when creating their music. The New York production duo of Tim Goldsworthy and James Murphy—aka DFA (short for Death From Above, or Don't Fucking Ask)—have long cited the drum speed and the drum production of Hannett's Joy Division as a crucial influence. In their band guise, LCD Soundsystem, James Murphy even lists a long line of artists he has always considered cool. On 'Losing My Edge', from their eponymous debut album of 2005, he can be heard to chant "Pere Ubu, Gil Scott-Heron, Joy Division, The Sonics" among others.

Radio 4, who have themselves been touched by the production genius of the DFA team, are also well aware of the significance of a prominent snare sound or trebly hi-hat. Marc Riley of The Fall and the BBC, notes their debt to Joy Division. "The bottom line is that [Joy Division] were guys who'd gotten involved with another guy who was coming from a dark place. But they were into punk rock and they were playing it, and the image was just steered in a different direction. And if you look at the bands that followed, like Radio 4, like Interpol, they're the same kind of thing, all dark uniforms, all starting their songs with a rumbling bassline."

In 2005, many bands emerging from the UK or the USA could be said to have Joy Division influences. British act Kasabian, with their fusion of big-beat rhythms and catchy choruses, seem keen to play up their idolising of Joy Division, and fellow Brits The Rakes are more wiry, angular and frenetic than Curtis ever was. The Forest, a trio from Manchester whose line-up includes one of the sons of a member of The Fall, seem intent on drilling the listener into submission with a bassline patently borrowed from Hook. Even America's Black Rebel Motorcycle Club have employed that swaying, mammoth band noise that refuses to be argued with.

Away from the lingering echoes of Joy Division's music, the continuing relevance of the band has been marked by the emergence of a UK film with a working title of *Control*. It's said to have involvement from photographer Anton Corbijn and countless Manchester 'faces', all with varying degrees of relevance to the band's history. For a while the film looked as if it might not go ahead or was, at various points, to be about different aspects of their life, depending on whom you spoke to. To this confusion can be added the usual time-consuming problems associated with making any film, and questions of accuracy and a city already divided over all things Factory.

Chris Hewitt, who was approached to offer guidance by members of the script-writing team and those responsible for authenticity, holds a somewhat pessimistic view of the proposed work.

"The whole Manchester scene then *was* interesting, but I don't think it's legendary, and I think it's going to be very difficult to make an interesting movie about such a short span of musical history, unless they do Ian Curtis growing up. And is that of any interest to anybody?"

Hewitt also had some pointers as regards accuracy, but these were apparently not taken on board. "I went to a meeting with them. They'd invited people like John Robb (*UK writer and broadcaster*), Andy Rourke from The Smiths, quite a few others, to meet the film people.

"John and I were sat there talking to them about things that could be useful to them, thinking they would scribble down notes or run a dictaphone. John said that when he was in The Membranes he went to see Joy Division in the Imperial Hotel in Blackpool, and he said the actual feel of the hotel now (because he still goes back) is pretty much as it was back then.

"I said it would be great to recreate the Electric Circus for the film, but you'd have to find some real fleapit, paint it black and make it all smelly and dank. There's lots of pictures in existence, so you could do that. The Derby Hall in Bury where they played with the guy from Crispy Ambulance (*Alan Hempstall*) on vocals—that's known as Bury Met now, but it's still pretty much as it was. And I told them how the Cargo Studios they used in 24 Hour Party People had been re-opened, because they'd recently sold it—it's still pretty much the same as it was when Joy Division used it. But they didn't write any of it down."

Ah yes, 24 Hour Party People—the film that tried to tell the whole story. It was destined to fail. Romantic notions, misplaced memories and personal vendettas all clouded the critical opinion of the film on its release in 2002. Much of the debate was justified, and with a running time apparently cut down from three hours, many Joy Division fans concluded that a great deal of the band's history must have been left on the cutting-room floor. (A selection of off-cuts later surfaced on a bonus disc of the DVD release.) That said, the actor who played Ian Curtis (Sean Harris) did so with unnerving accuracy and respect.

In other film-related matters, dance artist Moby is rumored to be working as musical director on a biopic of Ian Curtis (based on Debbie Curtis' book *Touching From A Distance*) that's being produced by Amy Hobby (of *Secretary* fame). He's said to be compiling an album of Joy Division cover versions, all specially recorded.

The New Yorker made his love of the band known as long ago as 1995, when he contributed his own heavy, guitar-laden version of 'New Dawn Fades' to the Joy Division tribute album, *A Means To An End*, on Virgin Records. (The collection also featured Low, Girls Against Boys and Tortoise among others.) He then recorded another version of the song (with Peter Hook on bass) for the 24 Hour Party People soundtrack (2002), and performed it—again with Hook plus members of

Red Hot Chili Peppers and Smashing Pumpkins—at an LA festival in 2004. Last but not least, he finished his 2003 Glastonbury set with a cover of 'Love Will Tear Us Apart'.

But the fact that each new generation still buys its own Joy Division records is most significant of all. Sure, some are drawn to the enigma of Ian Curtis, and others may then forget the band, but many will go on to become interested in New Order, or club culture, or electronic music itself. All these routes are traceable back to Factory and Manchester.

The Unknown Pleasures of the modern age...

Not surprisingly, most writings on Joy Division's debut in the 25-plus years since its release have been increasingly warm. Each year brings new accolades, new nuances and new revelations. Has the myth now overtaken the facts? Can anyone really tell us why *Unknown Pleasures* still sounds so good, or even so different?

Many have tried. Jason Ankeny, in an online posting, claims that the individuality of the record can be traced to "the taut, visceral energy of the group's evolving sound" and observes that it "is informed by a sense of punk-influenced aggression absent from [their] later work..."

The word 'visceral' creeps in a few times in modern reviews of the record. But where does such emotion come from? Hannett's production is often cited as some kind of gate to the instincts of the musicians, as one anonymous review on the mp3.com website asserts. "[It emphasizes] the space in the most revelatory way since the dawn of dub—as much a hallmark as the music itself... something, somehow, seems to wait or lurk beyond the edge of hearing."

The press were realizing the significance of *Unknown Pleasures* as early as 1982, even solely within the context of Joy Division's work. As a *Trouser Press* review acknowledged: "[it] remains the band's most fully realised work... [it] is fired with the energy and excitement of the band set free in the studio for the first time..."

Perhaps the pressures of the modern age make the escape that *Unknown Pleasures* offers all the more appealing. Where once punk was the refuge of the few, perhaps nowadays the increasing numbers of people seeking a dose of the 'real' or 'non-corporate' can find it in this album. One post on the popular Drowned In Sound website would seem to concur...

"I'd be lost to the world, missing my bus stops, hunched in my seat, my mind wandering the gothic mansion in 'Day Of The Lords', when I'd realise I'd ended up miles and streets from my house, yet it didn't matter, I'd have all the more time to wander the greyness, just to listen to the album..."

Elsewhere a visitor to the BBC's Collective website in 2003 confessed that, although they'd had reservations about buying the album that year, it had since become a firm favorite. "To begin with it was alien and slightly intimidating; now it is the most human comfort I could ever consider."

What it is that draws these new admirers to the band remains unclear. Perhaps it goes back to the short length of time in which they operated, or the stark imagery with which their product is packaged. Perhaps artists think there is some secret to be unlocked somewhere in their story, or in the tragedy of their singer. Maybe Joy Division just have a lot more fans nowadays. Maybe it shouldn't be pinned down.

epilogue

Top Ten Joy Division Rarities

The short recording life of Joy Division makes the list of their most desirable releases all the more interesting, particularly as the loose nature of their contract with Factory Records meant their music could be released on other labels. The French Sordide Sentimental single, for example, would be highly sought after even if it only contained two tracks unavailable elsewhere, but its limited run of just 1,578 copies makes it even rarer and thus very expensive, and nowadays copies rarely surface on the open market.

Enigma PSS 139
An Ideal For Living
('Warsaw'/'No Love Lost'/'Leaders Of Men'/'Failures')
(EP, 1000 only, 14"x14" foldout picture sleeve, 6/78)
£600

Sordide Sentimental 33002
Licht Und Blindheit
('Atmosphere'/'Dead Souls')
(France, 1,578 only, fold-out sleeve, 3/80)
£400

Anonymous ANON 1
An Ideal For Living
('Warsaw'/'No Love Lost'/'Leaders Of Men'/'Failures')

(12″ EP reissue, 9/78)
£400

Virgin VCL 5003
Short Circuit: Live At The Electric Circus
(Includes 'At A Later Date', 10″ LP, orange vinyl, 6/78)
£80

Virgin VCL 5003
Short Circuit: Live At The Electric Circus
(Includes 'At A Later Date', 10″ LP, yellow vinyl, 6/78)
£50

Factory FAC 2
A Factory Sample
(2x7″ EP doublepack, includes 'Digital' and 'Glass', with a
set of five stickers, 1/79)
£40

Factory FACT 40
Still
(2-LP in hardback hessian sleeve with card inners and white
ribbon, 10/81)
£40

Factory FAC 2
A Factory Sample
(2x7″ EP doublepack, includes 'Digital' and 'Glass', without
the five stickers, 1/79)
£30

London 828968-2
Heart & Soul
(4-CD box set, with booklet, 12/97)
£25

Factory FACT 37
Here Are The Young Men
(VHS, 8/82)
£20

Warsaw/Joy Division Gigography

In just short of three years, Joy Division played more than 150 gigs. The dates below are confirmed to have taken place, through posters, tickets stubs or personal recollections. Where the support or headline act is unknown, no name has been entered.

1977 (as Warsaw)

29 May
Electric Circus, Manchester
Supporting Buzzcocks and Penetration. A poster for this concert advertised the band as Stiff Kittens, although the band insist they were known as Warsaw at the concert

31 May
Rafters, Manchester
Supporting Johnny Thunders & The Heartbreakers

1 Jun
The Squat, Manchester

2 Jun
Newcastle (venue unknown)

3 Jun
The Squat, Manchester
Supporting The Drones and The Negatives with The Worst and Reform

16 Jun
The Squat, Manchester
Supporting Harpoon Gags, Bicycle Thieves and The Spilt Beans

June
The Squat, Manchester (various dates)
These dates were played with Tony Tabac on drums

30 Jun
Rafters, Manchester
Supporting Generation X

July
The Squat, Manchester (various dates)

27 Aug
Eric's, Liverpool

August
Electric Circus, Manchester (date unconfirmed)

14 Sep
Rock Garden, Middlesbrough

24 Sep
The Electric Circus, Manchester
Supporting The Rezillos

2 Oct
Electric Circus, Manchester
The famous closing of the venue, recorded for the memorial album

7 Oct
Salford College of Technology
Supporting Slaughter & The Dogs, The Drones, Fastbreeder and V2

8 Oct
Manchester Polytechnic

13 Oct
Rafters, Manchester
Supported by The Yachts

19 Oct
Pips Disco, Manchester

24 Nov
Rafters, Manchester
Supported by The Heat and Accelerator

December

Rafters, Manchester (date unconfirmed; confusion exists)

31 Dec

The Swinging Apple, Liverpool

The final gig as Warsaw

1978 (Joy Division)

25 Jan

Pips Disco, Manchester

Supported by Connection. Billed as Warsaw in error

14 Mar

Bowdon Vale Youth Club, Altrincham

Supported by Staff 9

28 Mar

Rafters, Manchester (appearance unconfirmed)

The Zones and Winners also on bill

14 Apr

Rafters, Manchester

The Stiff and Chiswick label event. Joy Division appear after midnight to their annoyance.

20 May

Mayflower Club, Manchester

Supporting Emergency with The Risk

9 Jun
The Factory, Manchester
Supported by Pete Shelley's Tiller Boys, Durutti Column and Cabaret Voltaire

June
Band On The Wall, Manchester (date unconfirmed)

15 Jul
Eric's, Liverpool

27 Jul
Roots Club, Leeds
Supported by Durutti Column

28 Jul
The Factory, Manchester
Supporting Suicide with The Actors

29 Aug
Band On The Wall, Manchester

4 Sep
Band On The Wall, Manchester

9 Sep
Eric's, Liverpool
Supporting Tanz Der Youth

10 Sep
Royal Standard, Bradford
Supported by Emergency

20 Sep
Granada TV's *Granada Reports*
Performing 'Shadowplay'

2 Oct
Institute of Technology, Bolton

12 Oct
Kelly's, Manchester
Supported by The Risk

October
Band On The Wall, Manchester (date unconfirmed)

20 Oct
The Factory, Manchester
Supporting The Tiller Boys and Cabaret Voltaire

24 Oct
The Fan Club, Leeds
Supporting Cabaret Voltaire

4 Nov
Eric's, Liverpool

14 Nov
The Odeon, Canterbury

15 Nov
Brunel University, Uxbridge

19 Nov
Bristol (venue unconfirmed)

20 Nov
Check Inn Club, Altrincham
Supported by Bidet Boys and Surgical Spirits

26 Nov
New Electric Circus, Manchester
Supported by The Passage

1 Dec
Salford College of Technology
Supporting Ed Banger with Fast Cars

22 Dec
Revolution Club, York
Supported by Cabaret Voltaire

27 Dec
Hope And Anchor, London

1979

10 Feb
Bolton (venue unconfirmed)

16 Feb
Eric's, Liverpool
Supported by Cabaret Voltaire

28 Feb
Playhouse, Nottingham

1 Mar
Hope And Anchor, London

4 Mar
Marquee, London
Supporting The Cure

13 Mar
Band On The Wall, Manchester

17 Mar
University of Kent, Canterbury (concert unconfirmed)

30 Mar
Youth Centre, Walthamstow, London
Supported by Mark Houserde

3 May
Eric's, Liverpool
Supported by The Passage and Fireplace

11 May
The Factory (Russell Club) Manchester
Supported by John Dowie, A Certain Ratio and OMD

17 May
Acklam Hall, London

23 May
Bowdon Vale Youth Club, Altrincham

7 Jun
The Fan Club, Leeds

13 Jun
The Factory (Russell Club) Manchester

16 Jun
The Odeon, Canterbury
Supporting The Cure

17 Jun
Royalty Theatre, London
Supporting John Cooper Clarke

19 Jun
Lancaster University
Supporting John Cooper Clarke

22 Jun
Good Mood, Halifax

25 Jun
Free Trade Hall, Manchester
Supporting John Cooper Clarke and Fashion

June
Band On The Wall, Manchester (date unconfirmed)

28 Jun
The Factory (Russell Club), Manchester
Supporting Suicide

3 Jul
Free Trade Hall, Manchester

5 Jul
Limit Club, Sheffield
Supported by John Dowie and one other Factory artist

11 Jul
Roots Club, Leeds

13 Jul
The Factory (Russell Club), Manchester

20 Jul
Granada TV's *What's On*
Played 'She's Lost Control' against the famous 'cityscape' backdrop

27 Jul
Imperial Hotel, Blackpool
Supported by OMD and The Final Solution

28 Jul
The Mayflower Club, Manchester
The 'Stuff The Superstars' festival organised by City Life *magazine.*
Also appearing were The Fall, The Distractions, Psychedelic, John The
Postman, The 5 Skinners, Frantic Elevators, Armed Force, Elti Fits, The
Hamsters and Gordon The Moron (as compere)

2 Aug
YMCA, Prince Of Wales Conference Centre, London
Supporting The Monochrome Set with The Teardrop Explodes

8 Aug
Romulus Club, Birmingham
Supporting Dexy's Midnight Runners

11 Aug
Eric's, Liverpool
Supporting Swell Maps. Two performances

13 Aug
Nashville Rooms, London
Supporting OMD and A Certain Ratio

22 Aug
Youth Centre, Walthamstow, London

27 Aug
Open Air Festival, Leigh
Highlights came from members of the Zoo Records and Factory label rosters on this day only

31 Aug
The Electric Ballroom, London
Supported by Scritti Politti, The Monochrome Set and A Certain Ratio

8 Sep
Futurama One Festival, Leeds
Also appearing were Cabaret Voltaire, PiL, The Fall, Hawkwind, Echo & The Bunnymen, The Teardrop Explodes, Spizz Energi, OMD and more

14 Sep
Rock Garden, Middlesbrough (concert unconfirmed)

15 Sep
Something Else, BBC2
TV appearance, playing 'Transmission' and 'She's Lost Control'

22 Sep
Nashville Rooms, London

28 Sep
The Factory (Russell Club), Manchester
Supported by The Teardrop Explodes and Foreign Press

2 Oct
Mountford Hall, Liverpool
Supporting Buzzcocks

3 Oct
Leeds University
Supporting Buzzcocks

4 Oct
City Hall, Newcastle
Supporting Buzzcocks

5 Oct
Apollo, Glasgow
Supporting Buzzcocks

6 Oct
Odeon, Edinburgh
Supporting Buzzcocks

7 Oct
Capitol, Aberdeen
Supporting Buzzcocks

8 Oct
Caird Hall, Dundee
Supporting Buzzcocks

16 Oct
Plan K, Brussels
Supported by Cabaret Voltaire

18 Oct
Bangor University
Supporting Buzzcocks

20 Oct
Loughborough University
Supporting Buzzcocks

21 Oct
Top Rank, Sheffield
Supporting Buzzcocks

22 Oct
Assembly Rooms, Derby
Supporting Buzzcocks

23 Oct
King George's Hall, Blackburn
Supporting Buzzcocks

24 Oct
The Odeon, Birmingham
Supporting Buzzcocks

25 Oct
St George's Hall, Bradford
Supporting Buzzcocks

26 Oct
Electric Ballroom, London
Supported by The Distractions and A Certain Ratio

27-28 Oct
Apollo, Manchester
Supporting Buzzcocks

29 Oct
De Montfort Hall, Leicester
Supporting Buzzcocks

30 Oct
New Theatre, Oxford
Supporting Buzzcocks

1 Nov
Civic Hall, Guildford
Supporting Buzzcocks

2 Nov
Winter Gardens, Bournemouth
Supporting Buzzcocks

3 Nov
Sophia Gardens, Cardiff
Supporting Buzzcocks. Concert cancelled

4 Nov
Colston Hall, Bristol
Supporting Buzzcocks

5 Nov
Pavilion, Hemel Hempstead
Supporting Buzzcocks

7 Nov
Pavilion, West Runton
Supporting Buzzcocks

9 Nov
Rainbow Theatre, London
Supporting Buzzcocks

10 Nov
Rainbow Theatre, London
Supporting Buzzcocks

15 Dec
Eric's, Liverpool
Supported by Section 25, two concerts in one day

18 Dec
Les Bains Douches, Paris

31 Dec
Warehouse, Oldham Street, Manchester
*Private party for Factory. Joy Division played for half an hour to 100
invited guests, along with other artists from the label*

1980

11 Jan
Paradiso, Amsterdam
*The support act, who were believed to be local, pulled out, leaving Joy
Division to experiment with two completely different set lists*

12 Jan
Paard Van Troje, The Hague

13 Jan
Doornroosje, Nijmegen

14 Jan
King Kong, Antwerp
Supported by De Kommeniste

15 Jan
The Basement, Cologne

16 Jan
Lantaren, Rotterdam

17 Jan
Plan K, Brussels
Supported by Digital Dance

18 Jan
Effenaar, Eindhoven

19 Jan
Club Vera, Groningen

21 Jan
Kant Kino, Berlin

7 Feb
The Factory (New Osborne Club), Manchester
Supported by A Certain Ratio and Section 25

8 Feb
University Of London Union
Supported by Killing Joke, Section 25, The Smirks and other uncon-firmed artists

20 Feb
Town Hall, High Wycombe
Supported by Killing Joke and Section 25

28 Feb
The Warehouse, Preston

29 Feb
The Lyceum, London
Supported by Killing Joke, A Certain Ratio and Section 25

5 Mar
Trinity Hall, Bristol
Supported by The Passage

2-4 Apr
The Moonlight Club, London
Supported by Section 25 on all dates

4 Apr
Rainbow Theatre, London
Supporting The Stranglers with Section 25 and The Soul Boys

5 Apr
Winter Gardens, Malvern
Supported by The Primal Screamers and Section 25

8 Apr

Derby Hall, Bury

The infamous 'riot' gig with Alan Hempstall on vocals for part of the set. With The Minny Pops and Section 25

11 Apr

The Factory (New Osborne Club), Manchester

Supported by The Minny Pops

19 Apr

Ajanta Theatre, Derby

Supported by Section 25 and XL5

2 May

High Hall, Birmingham University

Supported by A Certain Ratio

appendix 1
singles discography

Date	Title	UK Label/ no
Oct 1979	Transmission	Factory Fac 13
April 1990	Love Will Tear Us Apart	Factory Fac 23
June 1980	Komakino	Factory Fac 28
Sept 1980 (US)	She's Lost Control	Rough Trade Factus 2
September 1980	Atmosphere	Facory Facus 2
1988	Atmosphere 1988	Factory Fac 213
May 1995	Love Will Tear Us Apart	London YOJX1

appendix 2
ep discography

appendix 3
album discography

Date	Title	UK Label / no.
June 1979	Unknown Pleasures	Factory FACT 10

Tracks:
Disorder
Day Of The Lords
Candidate
Insight
New Dawn Fades
She's Lost Control
Shadowplay
Wilderness
Interzone
I Remember Nothing

Date	Title	UK Label / no.
July 1980	Closer	Factory FACT 25

Tracks:
Atrocity Exhibition
Isolation
Passover
Colony
A Means To An End
Heart & Soul
24 Hours

The Eternal

Decades

<table>
<tr><td>October 1981</td><td>Still</td><td>Factory FACT 40</td></tr>
</table>

Tracks: Exercice One

Ice Age

The Sound of Music

Glass

The Only Mistake

Walked In Line

The Kill

Something Must Break

Dead Souls

Sister Ray

Ceremony (live)

Shadowplay (live)

A Means To An End (live)

Passover (live)

New Dawn Fades (live)

24 Hours (live)(unlisted)

Transmission (live)

Disorder (live)

Isolation (live)

Decades (live)

Digital (live)

<table>
<tr><td>July 1988</td><td>Substance 1977-1980</td><td>Factory FACT 250</td></tr>
</table>

Tracks: Warsaw

Leaders Of Men
Digital
Autosuggestion
Transmission
She's Lost Control
Incubation
Dead Souls
Atmosphere
Love Will Tear Us Apart

1990   Peel Sessions   Strange Fruit SFRLP 111

Tracks: Exercise One
            Insight
            She's Lost Control
            Transmission
            Love Will Tear Us Apart
            24 Hours
            Colony
            Sound Of Music

June 1995   Permanent 1995   London 828624-2

Tracks: Love Will Tear Us Apart
            Transmission
            She's Lost Control
            Shadowplay
            Day Of The Lords
            Isolation
            Passover

Heart and Soul

24 Hours

These Days

Novelty

Dead Souls

The Only Mistake

Something Must Break

Atmosphere

Love Will Tear Us Apart – Permanent

May 1999   Preston 28 February 1980

                                    Factory FACD2.60

Tracks: Incubation

                Wilderness

                24 Hours

                The Eternal

                Heart And Soul

                Shadowplay

                Transmission

                Disorder

                Warsaw

                Colony

                Interzone

                She's Lost Control

July 2000   The Complete BBC Recordings

                            Strange Fruit SFRSLP094

Tracks: Exercice One (John Peel Show 31 Jan 79)

                Insight (John Peel Show 31 Jan 79)

She's Lost Control
(John Peel Show 31 Jan 79)
Transmission
(John Peel Show 31 Jan 79)
Love Will Tear Us Apart
(John Peel Show 26 Nov 79)
Twenty Four Hours
(John Peel Show 26 Nov 79)
Colony (John Peel Show 26 Nov 79)
Sound of Music
(John Peel Show 26 Nov 79)
Transmission
(Recorded live for
Something Else 4 Sept 79)
She's Lost Control
(Recorded live for
Something Else 4 Sept 79)
Ian Curtis & Steven Morris
interviewed by R. Skinner

April 2001	Les Bains Douche	Factory FACD2.61

Tracks: Disorder
Love Will Tear Us Apart
Insight
Shadowplay
Transmission
Day Of The Lords
Twenty Four Hours
These Days

A Means To An End
Passover (Amsterdam, 11 January 1980)
New Dawn Fades
(Amsterdam, 11 January 1980)
Atrocity Exhibition
(Amsterdam, 11 January 1980)
Digital (Eindhoven 18 January 1980)
Dead Souls (Eindhoven 18 January 1980)
Autosuggestion
(Eindhoven 18 January 1980)
Atmosphere (Eindhoven 18 January 1980)

(Recorded at Les Bains Douches 18 December 1979)

index